The Then and Now Series

GW00372316

"OSCAR WILDE - THE TRAGEDY OF BEING EARNEST"

JEAN GRAHAM HALL
and
GORDON D. SMITH

Barry Rose Law Publishers Ltd
Chichester

The Then and Now Series No. 3

"Oscar Wilde -
The Tragedy of Being Earnest"

ISBN 1 902681 27 4

Published by
Barry Rose Law Publishers Ltd
Chichester, England

Jean Graham Hall
All Books Published by Barry Rose

With Barbara H. Mitchell
Child Abuse Procedures and Evidence, 1st Edition, 1978

With Douglas F. Martin
Crimes Against Children, 1992
Child Abuse Procedure and Evidence, 3rd Edition, 1993
Haldane - Statesman, Lawyer, Philosopher, 1996
A Perfect Judge - Cases and Reports of Lord Sterndale, Master of
  the Rolls, 1999

(In preparation)
Biography of Lord Schuster (Permanent Secretary to nine Lord
  Chancellors)

With Gordon D. Smith
The Expert Witness, 1992
The Expert Witness - 2nd Edition, 1997
The Expert Witness - 3rd Edition, 2001

The Then and Now Series
  No.1 - Bywaters and Thompson, 1997
  No.2 - The Croydon Arsenic Mystery, 1999

Gordon D. Smith
Contributor to *The Sunday Times Book of Olympics*, Ed. Norman
  Harris, 1972

Contents

"Oscar Wilde - The Tragedy of Being Earnest"

Foreword

More than a hundred years of apologia has contained many inaccurate comments upon the various legal processes in which Oscar Wilde became involved. In this, the third of our "Then and Now Series" we deal with some of the stultifying legal events and place them in context, and make a comparison with the legal setting today.

By far the most important difference between then and now is that the law has completely changed. Oscar Wilde could not today be charged with offences of gross indecency in private with a consenting male adult. That he committed those acts is not in issue. After the trials he freely admitted the offences in spite of vehemently denying them on oath in court. By knowingly and freely indulging in behaviour which he knew was criminal, Oscar Wilde was the author of his own destruction.

The title of this book reflects the fact that, according to Theo Aronson, the word "Earnest" became a synonym for "homosexual" in some circles in Britain during the 1880s. "Is he Earnest?" became a familiar question. Later this gave the title of Oscar Wilde's play *The Importance of Being Earnest"* not only a double but a treble meaning.

Jean Graham Hall
Gordon D. Smith

Acknowledgements

We wish to record our gratitude to a number of people and in particular to Robert Cook, Gregory Fox J.D., Joe Gordon, David Jones, Professor Frank Mort, Michael Seeney, the Secretary of the Oscar Wilde Society; also the Howard League for Penal Reform and the Prison Reform Trust.

"It is a sad and sobering statue, but like most good and great art, it is provocative. Looking at that statue, I see a face of misery and perhaps other things about the way in which we, as a society, have behaved. I see what we, as a society, did to an individual and have continued to do through much of this [ie, 20th] century. Our society has, I believe, been intolerant and hypocritical and has perpetuated the belief that the behaviour of such as Oscar Wilde was unnatural, wrong and by our standards, criminal."

(Mr Shaun Woodward MP (Witney) speaking in the House of Commons, January 25, 1999)

CHAPTER 1

Social Attitudes Towards Homosexuality

A well-known (no doubt apocryphal) story of some decades ago used to illustrate the hypocrisy and prudery of the English middle class, was of the child who piped up in the middle of a luncheon party of his parents: "What did Oscar Wilde go to prison for, Daddy?" Embarrassment all round, and a rapid change of subject.

The history of sexuality and of attitudes to sex has received considerable attention in academic circles and elsewhere in recent years, but the published works seem to have a greater emphasis on literary rather than historical aspects. Whilst not offering too heavy a dissertation on the subject, the authors feel, nonetheless, that it is important to try to give the 21st century reader some perspective on the reactions of educated people to the disclosure of the trials in the year 1895.

Henry VIII's schism with the Church of Rome had many peripheral effects: in 1533 the King of England issued a decree superseding Roman Ecclesiastical law bringing sodomy and buggery under the jurisdiction of the Civil Authorities.

According to Michael S. Poldy, historians who have studied same-sex passion have generally agreed in describing the boundaries between sex and gender as much more relaxed and fluid in early modern England than they were during the Victorian era. He goes on to suggest that while this largely held true for working class men throughout the 19th century "... social and cultural expectations regarding gender roles and sexual preferences for middle class men and women were becoming more rigidly drawn by the 18th century."[1] The "explosion" of inquiry in the 19th century led to the first scientific researches.

---

1. Michael S. Poldy, *The Trials of Oscar Wilde*, Yale University Press, 1997.

In Germany Karl Westphal described the same-sex passion as "contrary sexual sensation" in a paper published in 1869, whilst an Italian doctor coined the phrase: "an inversion of the sexual instinct" a few years later. Some authorities state that it was a Hungarian who first used the word "homosexual" ie, Karl Mario Kertberry (Benkert) in 1869. Theo Aronson claims that this word came "into general use" in Britain during the 1880s.[2] This seems unlikely as the *Oxford English Dictionary* credits one C.G. Chaddock a translator of "Psychopathia Sexualis" (see below) as the originator in 1892, particularly as the word was not adapted into the French until 1907; the most commonly used descriptions being pederast and sodomite, the latter adopted by the Marquis of Queenberry on his infamous card that triggered the trials.

Theories abound as to the causes and nature of "inversion". The best known work for many years was the *Psychopathia Sexualis* of Richard Krafft-Ebing (a neurologist from Germany 1840/1902) which remained an influential source until well into the 20th century. Krafft-Ebing considered that inversion was essentially inherited (as opposed to learned) ie, a disease that affected the nervous system, in fact a form of madness. As a result he distinguished this from other "psychopathologies" such as necrophilia, which he considered criminal acts. He felt so strongly about this that he lobbied accordingly for the repeal of anti-sodomy laws.

At about this time an Austrian lawyer and customs official, Karl Heinrich Ulrichs, had put forward a radically different theory. Ulrichs, whom Krafft-Ebing rather scathingly described as being "himself subject to this perverse instinct" affirmed that the sexual mental life was not connected with physical sex. He declared that there were males who seemed like women to other men which he described as a female soul in a male body. These he gave the name of "Urnings" in an elaborate male sexual classification he had devised. Normal men were dubbed "Diornings" with various other titles for males who preferred effeminate men, or powerful men, or adolescents and so on. This work was never translated into

---

2. Theo Aronson, *Prince Eddy and the Homosexual Underworld*, John Murray, 1994.

English, but the essence of his thought was disseminated in Britain in pamphlets written under the pseudonym of *Numa Numantius* and in John Addington Symond's *Problems in Modern Ethics* (1891) and by Havelock Ellis a year or so after the Wilde trials. Ulrichs was certainly ahead of his time in some respects "he ... demanded nothing less than the legal and social recognition of the sexual love of the Urnings as congenital and therefore as of right; and the permission of marriage (*sic*) among them."[3] However, Krafft-Ebing was dismissive: "Ulrichs failed however to prove that this certainly congenital and paradoxical sexual feeling was psychological and not pathological."[4]

A more bizarre theory, at least to people today, originated from a man described by Colin Wilson as one of the most brilliant scientists of the 19th century - Cesare Lombroso.[5] He studied thousands of criminals in his work as Medical Superintendent of an asylum at Pavia and later as professor of forensic medicine and psychiatry at Turin. He concluded that there is a criminal "type" of person who could be identified by statistical analysis of various physical aspects. He considered sexual inversion to be both criminal and pathological, a variety of "moral insanity" and that the born criminal possesses the ferocious instincts of primitive humanity. Accordingly he considered all criminals, including inverts, should be imprisoned and not be allowed to procreate. His best known work *L'Uomo Delinquente* was published in 1876, but in later years Lombroso modified his views considerably.

So much for medical/psychological theory, what about reality?

"Male homosexuality has certainly been prevalent in this country since the time of the Norman Conquest. At least four English Kings have been inverts, as also have been a number of distinguished soldiers, clergy, poets, peers of the realm, Members of Parliament and others prominent in one rank or other of English society." Thus H. Montgomery Hyde in 1948 in his edited edition of *The Trials of*

---

3. Dr Richard von Kraft-Ebing, *Psychopathia Sexualis*, Paperback Library Inc., New York, 1965.
4. Krafft-Ebing, *ibid.*
5. Colin Wilson, *Written in Blood*, Grafton Books, 1990.

Oscar Wilde.

Homosexual scandals have, of course, occurred over the centuries. The younger son of William the Conqueror, William Rufus, was refused a Christian burial after his early, and accidental, death, as his lifestyle had appalled many people. By the mid-nineteenth century scandal of this sort was not restricted to the high and mighty, and the growth of national newspapers in the succeeding years created a much wider awareness.

In 1850 the Master-General of the Royal Military Academy, Woolwich, created the very reverse effect from the one he no doubt wished to achieve by dumping 33 boys on their parents' doorsteps without warning accompanied only by a brief, non-specific note for their dismissal. The farcical atmosphere was increased by a letter to *The Times* from the father of one of the boys stating he had no idea what his son was supposed to have done.

Another case that had even more elements of pure farce, and received "enormous publicity" according to Neil Bartlett[6] was a charge against Mr Ernest Boulton and Mr Frederick Parke of "conspiracy to commit a felony". The two were well-known in society as Stella and Fanny, two transvestites who dressed in the height of (feminine) fashion. Thus attired, they had been driven in the Park, squired to first nights and expensive restaurants. On April 28, 1870 they were arrested as they emerged from the Strand Theatre, London. From a private box they had attracted much attention as a result of their extravagant conduct such as twirling their handkerchiefs and lasciviously ogling the male occupants of the stalls. After visiting the ladies' room they left the theatre and were arrested by the waiting police and charged with the misdemeanour of being men dressed in female attire. Next day they appeared at Bow Street Magistrates' Court. At their trial for conspiracy to commit a felony, ie, sodomite acts, held at Westminster Hall before the Lord Chief Justice, the evidence proved to be insufficient for a conviction. On their arrest Fanny and Stella had been examined for anal penetration but the medical evidence

---

6. Neil Bartlett. *Who was that Man?* Serpent's Tail. 1988, pp.131/133.

was confused and inconclusive. They were both found "not guilty".[7]

The trial added to the ground swell of public revulsion. This was to be magnified by two much more serious indications of degeneration in the mind of the general public, in 1884 and 1889. The first centred on Dublin Castle, the home of the British Government Administration in Ireland. A homosexual group including several senior members of the administration were exposed. Four men were tried and found guilty. The most severe sentence was imprisonment for 20 years. Certain sections of the public were outraged.

The following year the Criminal Law Amendment Act 1885 aimed principally at eliminating child prostitution, was before Parliament. It was only at the eleventh hour of the passage of the Bill, after the Second Reading, that Henry Labouchère's amendment was included:

> "Any male person who in public or private commits or is party to the commission of or procures or attempts to procure the commission by any male person of any act of gross indecency with another male person shall be guilty of a misdemeanour and being convicted thereof shall be liable at the discretion of the court to be imprisoned for any term not exceeding two years with or without hard labour" (see Chapter 5).

The famous Cleveland Street Affair some four years later illustrated the English capacity for hypocrisy and double standards. Disclosures were triggered by inquiries into a theft at the Central Telegraph Office: it emerged that some telegraph messenger boys had been employed in a male brothel patronised by, among others, Lord Arthur Somerset and the Earl of Euston. Lord Arthur was Extra Equerry to the Prince of Wales, and a Major in the Royal Horse Guards ("the Blues").

Only two men were arrested, an 18-year old clerk at the Telegraph Office and the partner of the owner of the brothel (who had absconded). They were duly sentenced in September 1889 to

---

7. Alan Sinfield. *The Wilde Century*. Cassell, 1994, p.6.

nine months' and four months' imprisonment respectively.

That same month the Prime Minister, the Marquis of Salisbury, received a letter from the Home Secretary, Sir Matthew White Ridley, stating that the Attorney-General agreed with the Director of Public Prosecutions that the case against Lord Arthur Somerset was complete: in fact, no action was taken until November 12 when a warrant was finally issued, several months after his Lordship - as was well known - had fled to France. Lord Euston and Lord Arthur were the subject of an exposé in a new newspaper, the *North London Press*, at this time. Lord Euston immediately sued the Editor for criminal libel: he did not deny that he had been to the Cleveland Street premises but only once and that had been a misunderstanding. The unfortunate editor, Mr Ernest Parke, was found guilty by a jury and received a sentence of 12 months' imprisonment.

Several features of this case must have left a permanent impression, not least the authorities' inexplicable delay in taking any positive action against Somerset.

In the first third of the nineteenth century more than 50 men were hanged for sodomy in England. In one year, 1806, there were more executions for sodomy than for murder, while in 1810 four out of five convicted sodomites were hanged. In 1841 Lord John Russell unsuccessfully attempted to remove "unnatural offences" from the list of capital crimes. The penalty was in fact in disuse after 1836, and was finally removed in 1861, to be replaced by sentences of between 10 years' and life imprisonment. It was to remain thus until 1967. On the passing of the Criminal Law Amendment Act 1885 all male homosexual acts, whether committed in public or private, were illegal.

"Homosexual" scandals, usually involving the aristocracy and upper classes, were well-known to the general public by late Victorian times. But how aware were they of homosexuality in ordinary life? Working class people no doubt had the "nous" engendered partly by living in overcrowded conditions. Some middle class men would have had a comprehension resulting from boarding school experiences, although the authors believe this was not so widespread as some people maintain - including Lord Alfred Douglas. In his *Autobiography* he explained that he had three types of relationships at Winchester - the perfectly wholesome and normal, others sentimental and passionate, and others again which were neither pure nor innocent. He added, significantly: "But if it is to be assumed from this that I was 'abnormal' or 'degenerate' or exceptionally wicked then it must also be assumed that at least 90 per cent of my contemporaries at Winchester and Oxford were the same."[8]

The authors' view is that the majority of people had only a hazy idea of homosexual love and behaviour, and almost certainly only limited understanding, at best.

Escort Agencies

At least five of the young men with whom Wilde became involved were introduced to him through Alfred Taylor, who lived at 13 College Street, Westminster. Wilde visited the premises and there met the various youths who frequented the house. These youths were eg, unemployed valets and grooms and were available for what would be termed "escort services" today.

After the committal proceedings against Wilde had commenced at Bow Street Magistrates' Court, and as a result of evidence given there by at least two of the young men, Taylor was arrested and stood trial with Wilde at the Old Bailey on counts of gross indecency and conspiring with Wilde to procure the commission of certain acts. At the first trial the jury could not agree on some of their verdicts and a second trial was ordered. The second trial of each of the accused took place separately as the charge of conspiracy had been dropped by the prosecution and there was no legal nexus between the two defendants.

They were sentenced together - each to two years' imprisonment with hard labour. In passing sentence Mr Justice Wills said that this was the worst case he had ever tried:

"That you, Taylor, kept a kind of male brothel it is impossible

---

8. Lord Alfred Douglas, *Autobiography*, Martin Secker, 1929.

to doubt. And that you, Wilde, have been the centre of a circle of extensive corruption it is equally impossible to doubt."[9]

Alfred Taylor, a product of Marlborough College, did not [in the view of the authors], keep a brothel in the strict sense of that word, ie, a house where prostitutes may be visited. It would appear that no sexual activities took place there between "clients" and the young men. Rather Taylor provided a service, ie, young men willing to take part in sexual activities elsewhere, could be procured there.

Today male brothels exist, operating in a "blind eye" world. They can be found through advertisements in certain gay men's magazines. Some knowledge of the nomenclature used is required. An agency which offers "Escort Services: massage, full treatment" would probably be a discreetly run house in a respectable neighbourhood such as in the vicinity of Earls Court Underground Station. If the neighbours make no complaint as to noise and any disturbance one could expect to find a number of young men available in a house run quietly and efficiently by a *maître d'*. The guest would be offered the choice of various young men (all over the age of 18) of different nationalities and physical type, some of whom are in London to "improve their English". Any meeting of the young men and the client outside of the "agency" is categorically discouraged. The cost could be £70 - of which £40 might go to the young man, and the residue to the house.[10]

Escort services - ie, meetings at the client's house or hotel, or at premises provided by the young men are also freely available through advertisements in the same magazines. Little seems to have changed in over a hundred years, save that the whole scene today has become much more open and explicit within the past 10-15 years.

---

9. H. Montgomery Hyde (ed), *The Trials of Oscar Wilde*, Hodge, 1948.
10. Information provided by a gay friend.

CHAPTER 2

Prosecution of Lord Queensberry for Criminal Libel

On February 18, 1895, the Marquess of Queensberry left a visiting card with the hall porter of the Albemarle Club, 13 Albemarle Street, Piccadilly, London, where both Mr and Mrs Wilde were members, on which he had written "For Oscar Wilde posing as a Somdomite" (*sic*). The porter put the card in an envelope without showing it to anyone until delivering it to Oscar Wilde on his next visit to the club on February 28, 1895. This was the culmination of a vendetta which Queensberry was conducting against Wilde. It had begun with a letter from the Marquess to Wilde, requesting Wilde to terminate his friendship with his son, Lord Alfred Douglas, at once, followed by visiting Wilde at his home. Frustrated at being ignored, Queensberry attempted to get a bouquet of carrots handed over the footlights to Wilde at the theatre before leaving the visiting card at Wilde's club.

Wilde consulted solicitors recommended to him by an old friend Robert Ross: Messrs C.O. Humphreys, Son and Kershaw. Lord Alfred Douglas and Ross accompanied him. Charles Humphreys asked Wilde if there was any truth in the libel. In reply Wilde gave a solemn assurance of his innocence.[1]

Later Sir Edward Clarke, QC, MP, a former Solicitor-General, offered to appear without fee on Wilde's behalf in proceedings which Wilde decided to instigate. He too questioned Wilde, stating that he could only accept the brief if there was no foundation for the

---

1. H. Montgomery Hyde. Ed. *Notable British Trials - The Trial of Oscar Wilde.* William Hodges 1948. Foreword - The Rt. Hon. Sir Travers Humphreys PC, p.3.

charges made against him. He too was assured that there was no vestige of truth in the allegation of sodomy and that the charges were absolutely groundless.[2]

A warrant was obtained for Queensberry's arrest. Queensberry was arrested, charged and committed from Great Marlborough Street Police Court for trial at the Central Criminal Court (the Old Bailey) arraigned on two counts of criminal libel.

Shortly before the trial, Wilde went to see his friend Frank Harris at the Café Royal, Regent's Street. Harris was the editor of the *Fortnightly Review,* and the two met frequently. On this particular occasion George Bernard Shaw was lunching with Harris.

Wilde was never a friend of GBS. They had met, on perhaps half a dozen occasions. Ernest Rhys (later to be the founding editor of the J.M. Dent *Everyman's Library Series*) describes how when they met at a social occasion in London, Wilde and Shaw "had a characteristic passage of arms, both gay and bitter."[3]

Harris used to entertain lavishly at the Café Royal, sending out invitations by telegrams, each as long as a letter, on the day of the luncheon.

On this particular occasion, just before the trial of Queensberry, Wilde came to the Café Royal to ask Harris if he would be a witness at the trial, testifying that *The Picture of Dorian Gray* was a moral story. Harris refused, warning Wilde that he was going to lose the case against Queensberry and that he should drop it at once:

> "You should go abroad and as ace of trumps, you should take your wife with you. Now for the excuse - I would sit down and write such a letter as you alone can do to *The Times.* You should set forth how you have been insulted by the Marquess of Queensberry and how you went naturally to the Court for a remedy, but you found out very soon that this was a mistake."[4]

---

2. Sheridan Morley, *Oscar Wilde,* Weidenfeld and Nicholson, 1975, p.108.
3. A.M. Gibbs. Ed. *Shaw. Interviews and Recollections* - University of Iowa Press. 1990. St John Ervine, p.507.
4. Frank Harris. *Oscar Wilde,* with a preface by Bernard Shaw. Constable 1938, p.142.

Harris recalled that Oscar seemed to be inclined to do as he proposed and Shaw said he thought Harris was right. At about that time Bosie Douglas came in and at Wilde's request Harris repeated his argument. Bosie got up, accusing Harris of being no friend of Oscar's and left the room. Wilde followed him saying, "It is not friendly of you, Frank."[5] Shaw assured Harris that he had nothing with which to reproach himself, and supports Harris's account of what transpired.[6]

Regina (Wilde) v. Queensberry

John Sholto Douglas, Marquess of Queensberry, was arraigned at the Central Criminal Court on two alternative counts:

1. Continuing and maliciously intending to injure Wilde and to incite him to commit a breach of the peace and to bring him into public contempt scandal and disgrace by publishing a false scandalous malicious and defamatory libel in the form of a card directed to Wilde - which had the meaning that Wilde had committed and was in the habit of committing the abominable crime of buggery.
2. Intending to deprive Wilde of his good name credit and reputation and to incite and provoke him to commit a breach of the peace and bring him into public contempt scandal and disgrace in that he wickedly wrote and published a false scandalous malicious and defamatory libel in the form of a card directed to Wilde to the great damage scandal and disgrace of Wilde.[7]

Queensberry pleaded not guilty and entered a written plea of justification claiming that the libel was true and that it was for the

---

5. *Ibid.* Preface xxvii.
6. Introduction to *The Dark Lady of the Sonnets.* 1914. Bernard Shaw.
7. H. Montgomery Hyde, p.107.

public benefit that it should be published.[8]

Criminal Libel in 1895

Mansfield CJ in *Thorley v. Lord Kerry* (1812) 4 Taunt 355, defined defamatory libel as containing

> "that sort of imputation which is calculated to vilify a man and bring him, as the books say, into hatred, contempt and ridicule."

A person who was seriously libelled, whether by publication to himself or to third parties, could himself take criminal proceedings against the libeller; alternatively he could invite the police or the Director of Public Prosecutions to do so. Both these bodies could exercise their discretion in deciding whether or not to prosecute.

Civil actions were not excluded or a bar to criminal proceedings. However, for an action of civil libel to succeed it had to be published to a third person.

The Libel Act 1843 provided that the statutory maximum punishment for the common law offence of defamatory libel should be two years' imprisonment if the accused, as in Count 1 of the Indictment against the Marquess of Queensberry, was proved to have known the falsity of the libel. In default of such proof the maximum punishment was one year's imprisonment.

The Libel Act 1843 (Lord Campbell's Act) also provided a new statutory defence to the charge of criminal libel, ie,

(a)   that what had been written was true and
(b)   it was for the public good that it should be written (Section 6).

Until the Act was passed, proof of the truth of the libel was no defence. The libel was a crime because it tended to cause a breach of peace. Hence the old adage: "the greater the truth the greater the

---

8.   *Ibid.*, p.108.

libel".

In *Boaler v. The Queen* (1888) 21 QBD 284, Field J said

> "It is clear, before Lord Campbell's Act 1843, that knowledge of the libel was immaterial in point of law although it might be of weight in the consideration of the punishment, as it is a great aggravation of a libel to publish it knowing it to be false. A defendant could not set up the defence that he did not know the libel to be false. Lord Campbell's Act gave him the right to plead that the libel was true and published for the public benefit."

In view of the part the "radical reformer" played in passing the infamous Section 11 of the Criminal Law Amendment Act 1885, see Chapter 5, it is interesting to note the case of *R. v. Labouchère* (1884) 12 QB 320. Labouchère was the proprietor of the newspaper *Truth* which contained the alleged libel. The offending article stated that the deceased father of the applicant, the Duke of Vallombrosa, not a resident in his country, had been

> "an army contractor who was nearly hanged on the charge of supplying meat to a French army corps, the flesh of soldiers who had died in hospital or had been killed in battle. Luckily for him the first Empire came to an end before the trial could take place, and the contractor having retired to Italy and purchased a dukedom, became a grand seigneur and an ardent adherent of the Bourbons."

This breath-taking allegation was never legally tested. An application was made under Section 8 of the Law of Libel Amendment Act 1888 to commence a prosecution against the proprietor of the newspaper. Lord Coleridge CJ refused leave to file a criminal information, *inter alia*, in respect of a libel upon a deceased person.

An indictment for criminal libel, as opposed to civil liability, was considered to be justified only where it affected the public as an attempt to disturb the public peace. "Libel is ranked among criminal offences because of its supposed tendency to arouse angry passion, provoke revenge and thus endanger the public peace" (*R. v. Holbrook* (1878) 4 QBD 42).

In *R. v. Adams* (1889) QBD Vol.22, p. 66, the defendant was tried and convicted on an indictment for criminal libel charging him with having unlawfully and maliciously written and published a defamatory letter to ESY a young lady of virtuous and modest character. The defendant, having seen an advertisement in a newspaper wrote to her saying:

> "I have seen your advertisement in the *Daily Telegraph*. I have no situation to offer you. I am a young man, 25 ... I should like to make certain proposals to you. Of course this is strictly private between you and I."

In the letter Adams, in very plain language, stated that if ESY was a virgin, he would offer her a sum of money to have intercourse with her. He also stated that perhaps one day she would lose her virginity for nothing.

Dismissing the appeal Lord Coleridge CJ said that the letter was a defamatory libel, tending to defame and bring into contempt the character of the person to whom it was sent. He was of the opinion that the letter was of such a character that it tended to provoke a breach of the peace.

Preliminary Proceedings

At the Great Marlborough Street Police Court on March 9, 1895, Mr Travers Humphreys appeared for Oscar Wilde; Mr E.H. Carson, QC, MP, and Mr C.F. Gill (instructed by Messrs Day and Russell) for the Marquess of Queensberry.[9]

Oscar Wilde gave his evidence and was then cross-examined by Mr Carson. However, the magistrate had no jurisdiction to receive evidence of the truth of the libel, even though Mr Carson indicated that justification was the plea Lord Queensberry would raise if the

---

9. *Ibid.*, p.31.

case was sent for trial. This procedure followed the case of *R. v. Sir Richard Carden* (1879) (LR 1880, Vol.V, p.1) in which the Court of Appeal held that the function of the magistrate was merely to determine whether there was such a case against the accused as ought to be sent for trial. The reason for the finding was given by Mr Justice Lush (p.12) who stated:

"Lord Campbell's Act of 1843 enabled the accused to know the truth of the libels, but only on certain conditions, ie, that he shall plead the truth specially to the indictment, and shall also allege that the publication of the libel was for the public benefit, and state the facts on which he relies to prove that it was so. Until those conditions are complied with, the truth of the libel cannot be rendered available to the defence, and consequently it is beyond jurisdiction of the magistrate to go into the question of its truth."

Trial at the Old Bailey

At the Old Bailey, Sir Edward Clarke, QC, MP, Mr Charles Matthews and Mr Travers Humphreys appeared for the prosecution - although Wilde was technically the prosecutor.

Sir Edward in his opening speech explained to the jury that the words of the libel were not directly an accusation of the "gravest offences" (ie, buggery). Rather:

"The suggestion was that there was no guilt of the actual offence, but that in some way or other the person of whom those words were written did appear - nay desired to appear - and pose to be a person guilty of or inclined to the commission of the gravest of all offences."[10]

Sir Edward continued:

---

10. *Ibid.*, p.108.

"You will appreciate that the leaving of such a card openly with the porter of a club is a most serious matter and one likely gravely to affect the position of the person as to whom that injurious suggestion was made."[11]

The plea of justification, filed on behalf of the defendant, named the persons with whom it was alleged Wilde had solicited and incited to commit sodomy and other acts of gross indecency and immorality, ie

Edward Shelley at the Albemarle Hotel, London
Sidney Mavor at the Albemarle Hotel, London
Frederick Atkins at 29 Boulevard des Capucines, Paris
Maurice Salis Schwabe at 29 Boulevard des Capucines, Paris
Alfred Wood at 16 Tite Street, London
Charley Parker at the Savoy Hotel, London
Edward Scarfe at 10 St James Place, London
Herbert Tankard at the Savoy Hotel, London
Walter Grainger at The Cottage, Goring, Oxfordshire
Alfonso Harold Conway at The Albion Hotel, Brighton.

Sir Edward explained that it was for those who had taken the responsibility of putting these serious allegations into the plea of justification to satisfy the jury if they could, by credible witnesses, that these allegations were true.[12]

At the end of the case for the prosecution, it was obvious to Sir Edward Clarke that the defence were in a position to call a number of witnesses named in the plea of justification, who would give evidence of a devastating nature so far as Oscar Wilde was concerned.

On the third day, during the opening speech for the defence by Mr Edward Carson QC, MP, Sir Edward Clarke conferred with Wilde. There was, said Sir Edward in some distress, no hope at all of a guilty verdict. If, moreover, the presence of Parker, Wood and

---

11. *Ibid.*
12. *Ibid.*, p.109.

the others on the witness stand was to be avoided, Wilde's charge would have to be withdrawn at once. There was then a chance that the matter would be allowed to drop, whereas if the men were called, Clarke now saw the arrest of Oscar as almost inevitable. Wilde agreed immediately.[13]

In court Sir Edward Clarke was seen to pluck Mr Carson's gown and the indulgence of the court was asked for while counsel consulted with one another. On counsels' return to the court, Mr Carson resumed his seat and Sir Edward addressed the Judge to say that he interposed to say on behalf of Mr Oscar Wilde that he would ask to withdraw the prosecution. If the Judge did not think he, Sir Edward, ought to do that, he was prepared to agree to a verdict of "Not guilty".

The Judge, Mr Justice Henn-Collins directed the jury to return a verdict of "Not Guilty". The jury retired to consider their verdict, and returned to find the Marquess of Queensberry "Not guilty" of criminal libel, having first found the plea of justification proved and that the alleged libel had been published for the public benefit.

H. Montgomery Hyde reminds us that it is difficult to visualise the strong public feelings and prejudices provoked by the Queensberry and Wilde trials. "Queensberry's acquittal was received with round after round of cheering in the court."[14] It was also obvious where public sympathy lay:

"The Judge did not attempt to silence or reprove the irrepressible cheering in the Court which greeted the acquittal of this sorely provoked and cruelly injured father. As for the prosecutor, whose notoriety had become so famous ... we have had enough of Mr Oscar Wilde who has been the means of inflicting on the public during this recent episode so much moral damage of the most hideous and repulsive kind as no single individual could well cause."

[*Daily Telegraph*, April 6, 1895]

---

13. Christopher S. Millard *Famous Old Bailey Trials of the XIX Century. Oscar Wilde. Three Times Tried.* Ferrestowe Press. 1912, p.124.
14. H. Montgomery Hyde. Introduction, p.11.

Sheridan Morley suggests that Wilde left only one real mystery behind him ie,

> "How could anyone with so well-developed a sense of his own image and importance of preserving it have failed to see the trap he was getting himself into until it was too late?"[15]

Morley avers that Wilde, advised by Robert Ross, went to the wrong solicitor when he received the card from the hall porter at the Albemarle Club; and that he should have gone to a lawyer such as Sir George Lewis (later retained by Queensberry) well versed in problems arising from the law's attitude to homosexuality.[16] Sir George might well have advised Wilde to take no further action. But would Wilde have followed that advice?

Heskett Pearson took the view that "Sir Edward Clarke's failure to show up Queensberry and then to put Douglas in the witness box, as he had promised to do, decided the verdict."[17]

In our opinion Pearson failed to grasp the essential elements of the law of criminal libel. The Marquess of Queensberry's character and his motive for publishing the libel were immaterial. Whether or not his son, Lord Alfred Douglas, would have cast doubt on his father's character if he had given evidence for the prosecution was of no consequence. The issues were clear and simple:

(1) Was what Queensberry wrote true?
(2) Was it for the public good that it should be written?

George Bernard Shaw, sympathetic to Wilde, may have reached the kernel of the truth:

> "When it became apparent that their client had no case at all, and that the defendant's case was overwhelming, Wilde had to surrender. I do not believe that he ever condescended to denials,

---

15. Sheridan Morley. *Oscar Wilde*. Weidenfeld and Nicolson, p.10.
16. *Ibid.*, p.107.
17. Heskett Pearson. *The Life of Oscar Wilde*. Methuen 1946, p.288.

except when legal fictions were necessary. Like most similarly afflicted men of culture, he was not only unashamed of his reversed sex instinct but proud of it, and its association with some great names."[18]

---

18. Frank Harris. *Oscar Wilde* with a Preface by Bernard Shaw. Preface. xxviii.

CHAPTER 3

Criminal Libel Today

Little has changed. Basically the law remains as it was in 1895. The Libel Act 1843 is still good law, and the legislation remains by which a person aggrieved by a serious defamatory libel can take criminal action.

One exception - The Faulks Committee on Defamation while considering the law of Criminal Libel in 1975 pointed out that by the decision in R. v. Wicks [1936] 1 AER 384 the tendency to disturb the peace need no longer be proved in order to support a criminal prosecution.[1]

Wicks had been concerned in litigation with an insurance company. In a letter to C, whom the company charged with an offence, Wicks published a defamatory libel concerning Q, the solicitor acting for the company. It was held, *inter alia*, that

(i)   the libel was not one which the jury would have been justified as regarding as trivial;

(ii) the prosecution was not bound to prove that the libel would have been unusually likely to provoke a breach of the peace.

On appeal Parcq J quoted Mansfield CJ in *Thorley v. Lord Kerry* and said:

"It is time that a criminal prosecution for libel ought not to be instituted, and if instituted, will probably be regarded with disfavour by the Judge and jury, when the libel complained of

---

1.   Report of the Committee on Defamation. Chairman: The Hon. Mr Justice Faulks. Cmnd. 5909, para.433.

is of so trivial a character or to be unlikely either to disturb the peace of the community or seriously to affect the reputation of the person defamed."

The Faulks Committee commented on the law in 1975 as follows:

"Criminal proceedings for libel should not be taken in trivial cases and juries may be directed by Judges to acquit in such cases. But, when the libel is serious, it is no defence for the libeller to show that the person he defames is unlikely to commit a breach of peace. It is however a defence to show that the libel was published on a privileged occasion. But there is singularly little authority on this matter."[2]

The Committee explained that a person who is seriously libelled, whether by publication to himself or third parties can, therefore, take criminal proceedings against the libeller or he may invite the police or the Director of Public Prosecutions to do so.

The Distinction between a Criminal Libel and a Civil Libel

In *Goldsmith v. Sperrings Ltd* [1977] (CA) 1 WLR Lord Denning made the distinction between criminal libel and civil libel.

"A criminal libel is so serious that an offender should be punished for it by the State itself. He should either be sent to prison or made to pay a fine to the State itself. Whereas a civil libel does not come up to that degree of enormity. The wrongdoer has to pay full compensation in money to the person who is libelled and pay for his costs; and he can be ordered not to do it again. But he is not to be sent to prison for it nor pay a fine to the State. When a man is charged with criminal libel, it is for the jury to say on which side of the line it falls. That is to say, whether or not it is so serious as to be a crime. They are

---

2. *Ibid.*, para.444.

21

entitled to, and should, give a general verdict of 'guilty' or 'not guilty'."

In *Gleaver v. Deakin* [1980] AC (H of L) 477, the House of Lords further explained that not every libel warrants a criminal prosecution. For this, the libel must be sufficiently serious to require the intervention of the Crown in the public interest.
As Lord Scarman said:

"The libel must be more than of trivial character; it must be such as to provide anger or cause resentment. The emphasis ... is upon the character of the language used. In my judgment, the references in the case-law to reputation, outrage, cruelty or tendency to disturb the peace are no more than illustrations of the various factors upon which writer alone or in combination contributed to the gravity of the libel. The essential feature of a criminal libel remains - as in the past - the publication of a grave, not trivial, libel."

The private prosecution in *Gleaver v. Deakin* had been brought against the authors and publishers of a book entitled *Johnny Go Home* in respect of allegations made against the prosecutor. During the committal proceedings at Wells Street London Magistrates' Court the defendants sought to adduce evidence that at the time of publication Gleaver had a bad reputation for violence and homosexual offences, and included evidence of his convictions for such offences. The purpose was to show that the alleged libel could not seriously affect his actual reputation and therefore was not so serious as to require the intervention of the State by way of criminal proceedings.

The House of Lords held that an examining magistrate, if satisfied that the libel has been published and is serious, must commit the defendant, leaving to the jury at trial the issue of public benefit, which includes questions as to truth and as to the character and reputation of the person defamed.

Their Lordships voiced general disquiet with the present law of criminal libel. Lord Diplock said that dealing with the legal characteristics of the criminal offence of defamatory libel left him:

"With the conviction that this particular offence has retained anomalies which involve serious departures from accepted principles upon which the modern criminal law of England is based and are difficult to reconcile with the international obligations which this country has undertaken by becoming a party to the European Convention for the Prosecution of Human Rights and Fundamental Freedoms."

The Law Lords agreed that it would be a salutary reform in the law of defamation if no prosecution for criminal libel could be instituted without leave of the Attorney General.

On this point Lord Edmund Davies commented:

"I abstain from ventilating at length such views as I entertain regarding the desirability of law reform in the matter of criminal libel. For this may well be regarded as not a wholly suitable occasion to do so, and even if it be, the most zealous law reformer must be discouraged by the well-nigh total apathy that has reigned since the publication in 1975 of the stimulating report of the Committee on Defamation (Cmnd 5909) presided over by Faulks J. It has indeed been strongly urged in some quarters that proceedings for criminal libel, rarely resorted to, should be abolished all together."

Few prosecutions for criminal libel have taken place in recent years. One of the more sensational was *Goldsmith v. Pressdram Ltd* [1977] QB 83, against the publishers of *Private Eye* for an alleged libel published by them concerning the latest incident in the continuing mystery of the disappearance of Lord Lucan. *Private Eye* recounted that the morning after the murder of Sandra Rivett, the Lucan nanny, a lunch was held by Lord Lucan's friend John Aspinall, who invited the Lucan circle so that they could decide what to do if Lucan turned up. The luncheon party included Jimmy Goldsmith, the Old Etonian reputedly a billionaire.

The article in *Private Eye* concluded thus:

"Goldsmith, the richest most powerful member of this group, is a man who is known both for his generosity towards his friends and dependants and for his ability to make them frightened of him."

A private apology had been made by the respondents who admitted that the libel contained in the article was not true and that Mr Goldsmith was not present at Mr Aspinall's luncheon party. In making this apology, the defendants accepted that they were mistaken. Wien, J., in his judgment said that this was a proper case for the criminal law to be invoked.

Recent Proposed Changes in the Law

The Faulks Committee had come to the conclusion that the fact that there are few prosecutions for libel does not mean of itself that the offence should be abolished. "The law which protects some people, if only a few, from injury should not be discarded unless there is something better to put in its place."[3]

The Director of Public Prosecutions agreed with them and stated, in a memorandum to the Committee:

"Rare though criminal proceedings may be in practice, the liability to such proceedings has I think a deterrent effect."

The Faulks Committee had recommended only slight alterations to the existing law, eg, courts of summary jurisdiction should be empowered to try cases of criminal libel with the consent of the defendant. Nothing has been done in this respect. If, therefore, the circumstances of the trial of the Marquess of Queensberry took place today, it would still be on indictment in a Crown Court.

The Law Commission published a Working Paper on the law of criminal libel in 1982 and was more radical in its approach than the Faulks Committee.[4] The Commission provisionally proposed the

---

3. *Ibid.*, para.446.
4. Law Commission Working Paper No.84. Criminal Libel. HMSO 1982.

abolition of the offence and in its stead recommended that a new statutory offence, ie, of publishing a statement about another person which is both untrue and defamatory and which the alleged libeller knows or believes to be untrue and which he intends should defame.

The new offence would be very much narrower than the prevailing law. "It is intended to penalise only the deliberate "character assassin", namely a person who makes or publishes a statement about another person which is both untrue and defamatory and which he knows or believes to be untrue and he intends should defame." This recommendation, made as part of the Law Commission's codification of the criminal law, has never been put into effect.

In 1991, in a Report of the Working Group of the Supreme Court Procedure, Chairman Neill LJ, one of a total of 26 recommendations dealing with the Rules of the Supreme Court in Defamation proceedings was that:

> "Parliament should consider whether the public interest required the retention of criminal libel at all, and if it does, should proceedings only be launched on the fiat of the Attorney-General."[5]

The Defamation Act 1996 - an Act to amend the law of defamation and to amend the law of limitation with respect to actions for defamation or malicious falsehood stated in Section 20(2):

> "Nothing in this Act affects the law relating to criminal libel."

The Bill commenced in the House of Lords. On the second reading in March, 1996, Lord Williams of Mostyn, a barrister with a considerable defamation practice, asked the question:

> "In 1996 is criminal libel appropriate to be kept as part of our law in any circumstances? Most commentators would think that it

---

5. Report of the Supreme Court Procedure Committee on Practice and Procedure in Defamation. 1991, Section IV, p.5.

had long outlived its usefulness."[6]

The matter was not pursued although at the end of the debate Lord Williams raised it again. The House of Commons then debated the Bill on second reading at some length but without any reference to criminal libel.

---

6. Parliamentary Debates (Hansard) House of Lords 5th Series, 1996, Vol.570, col.582.

CHAPTER 4

Arrest at the Cadogan Hotel

On the collapse of his criminal libel prosecution against the Marquess of Queensberry, Oscar Wilde left the Old Bailey on April 5, 1895, about noon. Together with Lord Alfred Douglas and Robert Ross he went first to the Holborn Viaduct Hotel in the vicinity of the Central Criminal Court and ultimately to the Cadogan Hotel in Sloane Street. There he was arrested by two police officers from Scotland Yard about 6.30 p.m.

In the meantime on the same day Charles Russell, solicitor for the Marquess of Queensberry, sent copies of relevant papers, ie, statements of witnesses for the defence together with shorthand notes of the trial to the Director of Public Prosecutions, Sir Hamilton Cuffe. These were also put before the Home Secretary Mr Asquith, and the Law Officers Sir Robert Reid and Sir Frank Lockwood in the House of Commons. On their instructions at about 3.30 p.m., a warrant for Wilde's arrest was applied for at Bow Street Magistrates' Court.

H. Montgomery Hyde discussed the timing of events:

"It had been said that the magistrate was careful to inquire the time of the boat train's departure from the clerk of the court and, as receiving this information, to have fixed the time of the application a quarter of an hour later."[1]

What is known as a fact is that it was not until after 5 p.m., by which time it is alleged the train had gone, that the magistrate signed a warrant for Wilde's arrest.

Travers Humphreys, junior counsel for Wilde who, like his

---

1. H. Montgomery Hyde. *Oscar Wilde - A Biography*. Eyre Metheun. 1976, p.224.

leader, Sir Edward Clarke, QC, had a complementary brief throughout the proceedings, believed that:

> "Wilde was given every opportunity to leave the country but elected to stay or more accurately he could not make up his mind to go, though he drew money from his bank and had his bag half-packed to go when he was arrested late in the afternoon. The authorities would, I believe, have been quite willing that he should go abroad, but since he did not avail himself of the delay in issuing the warrant, his prosecution was inevitable."[2]

On the other hand, having sat as a stipendiary magistrate at Bow Street for 18 months, one of the present authors, less romantic than the other, finds some difficulty in accepting the proposition that Sir John Bridge deliberately slowed down the process of granting the warrant in order to give Wilde time to make his escape abroad.

The magistrate, before issuing the warrant, would have had to finish or at least adjourn the case on which he was currently adjudicating and, before granting the warrant in chambers, would have wished to read the papers thoroughly, check them with his clerk to make sure they were in proper legal order, perhaps have a cup of tea in private while thinking the whole matter over before putting his signature to what he must have known was an application which would attract much publicity. The magistrate would be far more concerned with the correctness and authenticity of the process than with the social consequences.

What is certain is that Wilde's solicitors, when first advising him, had not the faintest idea that Wilde had laid himself open to the charges of gross indecency upon which he was ultimately convicted. In giving to his solicitors, as he afterwards admitted, his solemn assurance of his innocence, Wilde lied, as did Bosie Douglas.

In *De Profundis* Wilde admits to have found pleasure in entertaining the rent boys he met through Bosie and Alfred Taylor - later to be a co-defendant of Wilde:

---

2. H. Montgomery Hyde. *The Trials of Oscar Wilde*. William Hodge. 1946. Foreword by the Rt. Hon. Sir Travers Humphreys PC, p.2.

"They, from the point of view which I as an artist in life approached them, were delightfully suggestive and stimulating. It was like feasting with panthers. The danger was half the excitement. I used to feel as the snake-charmer must feel when he lures the cobra to stir from the painted cloth or reed basket at his bidding ... They were to me the brightest of the painted snakes."[3]

He goes on to say that what was loathsome to him was the memory of interminable visits to the solicitor Humphreys, in the presence of Bosie, in a ghastly bleak room, looking at a bald-headed man.

Bosie's account, however, is quite different. He contended that he had Wilde's assurances that the suggestions and accusations were untrue and he had not the smallest of reason to suppose that Wilde was lying to him.[4] "Believing him to be an innocent man, I told him that he was a fool to worry and that it was the other side who ought to be worrying ..."[5]

Wilde was a liar. He lied to his solicitor, to his barrister and to the courts on oath. Bosie was also a liar. He visited Alfred Taylor's male brothel at 13 Little College Street, Westminster and there procured rent boys for Wilde. Furthermore, there was evidence that he shared a bedroom with one of the boys at the Savoy Hotel while Wilde was also sharing another bedroom. George Bernard Shaw comments in a more kindly way:

"Wilde must have formally presented himself as innocent to his lawyers in his attack on Queensberry; otherwise they could not have taken his case into court ..."[6]

Shaw surmised that Wilde miscalculated the force of social vengeance he was unloosening on himself and how insanely he had been advised in taking the action.

---

3. *De Profundis*. Harper Collins. 1994, p.1042.
4. Lord Alfred Douglas. *Oscar Wilde and Myself.* John Long. 1914, p.95.
5. *Ibid.*, p.100.
6. Frank Harris. *Oscar Wilde.* Constable 1938. Preface by Bernard Shaw, p.xxviii.

Lord Alfred Douglas Not Charged

Alfred Taylor was charged with conspiracy and also with committing acts of indecency, and became a co-defendant. No criminal proceedings were commenced against Bosie Douglas.

We are not able to state categorically whether Oscar Wilde and Bosie Douglas had sexual relations with one another. However, there is little doubt that Bosie indulged in some same-sex acts before he met Oscar.

The Victorians loved sending telegrams, eg, Frank Harris used the telegram to summon guests to lunch at the Café Royal on the same day. To other men, with homosexual leanings, the popularity of the telegram had little to do with speed or convenience. They were interested in the messenger rather than the message, "These cheeky little lads in their tight blue uniforms and jauntily angled caps were welcomed - quite literally in some cases - with open arms."[7] Bosie is said to have been involved with a telegraph boy at Oxford, and because he was being blackmailed over this sought the acquaintance and advice of Wilde.

At the retrial of Wilde, the foreman of the jury interrupted the summing up of Mr Justice Wills to ask why Lord Alfred Douglas was not also on trial. The witnesses who had given evidence against Wilde could also have given evidence against Lord Alfred. Had a warrant even been issued for his apprehension? In reply, Mr Justice Wills said:

> "There is a natural disposition to ask, 'why should this man stand in the dock and not Lord Alfred Douglas?' It is a thing we can not discuss and to entertain any such consideration, as I have mentioned, would be prejudice of the worst possible kind."[8]

---

7. Theo Aronson. *Prince Eddy and the Homosexual Underworld*. John Murray, 1994, p.7.
8. Christopher S. Millard. *Famous Old Bailey Trials of the XIX Century. Oscar Wilde. Three Times Tried*. Ferrestowe Press. 1912, p.349.

In fact the Director of Public Prosecutions, Sir Hamilton Cuffe, had considered the matter. Before the trial of Oscar Wilde and Alfred Taylor he had sought the advice of Mr Charles Gill, senior treasury counsel. Recently, in December 1999, a letter written by Mr Gill to the DPP has come to light in the Public Records Office.[9] Mr Gill points out that Douglas was an undergraduate at Oxford when the two first met and in view of "the difference in their ages, and the strong influence that Wilde obviously exercised over Douglas since that time I think that Douglas may fairly be regarded as one of Wilde's victims."[10] There was also a lack of independent corroboration of evidence.

Bosie had left the country at Wilde's instigation and being out of the jurisdiction of the courts, it would have been impossible to execute any warrant. How much the fact that he was very well connected played in the DPP's decision not to prosecute can only be a matter of conjecture.

---

9. "Lost letter holds answer to riddle of Wilde trial." Peter Day and Catherine Milner. *Sunday Telegraph* December 28, 1999.
10. *Ibid.*

CHAPTER 5

Section Eleven - A Silent Passage Into Law

Following the collapse of his criminal prosecution against the Marquess of Queensberry, Oscar Wilde was charged with committing gross indecency with other male persons, contrary to Section 11 of the Criminal Law Amendment Act 1885.

Section 11 had a strange and silent passage into law. The original Bill contained no reference to indecency between males and had been introduced to deal with completely different circumstances.

Purpose of the Bill

The long title of the Criminal Law Amendment Act 1885 was "an Act to make further provision for the Protection of Women and Girls; the suppression of brothels, and other purposes." It came into force on January 1, 1886. The Bill was introduced in the House of Lords and in both Houses there were long, impassioned and sometimes acrimonious debates. Many members of each House wished to be heard on various aspects of the Bill such as the procuring or attempts to procure any woman or girl to become a common prostitute. One of the purposes of the Bill was to raise the age of female consent from the age of 13. Another was to curb the white slave traffic in girls sent to work in foreign brothels. Apart from section 11, dealing with "outrages on public decency", the Act has stood the test of time and has met with general approval and respect.

Section 11 dealt with an entirely different subject matter to the other sections of the Act, and had no nexus with them. Section 10 of the Act dealt with the power of search if there was reasonable cause to suspect that a girl or woman was detained for immoral purposes and Section 12 permitted the appointment of a guardian by the High Court of girls under 16 until the age of 21 where it was proved to the satisfaction of the court that the seduction or prostitution had been encouraged by a parent, guardian, master or mistress.

By Section 11 -

"Any male person who, in public or private commits or is a party to the commission of, or procures the commission by any male person, of any act of gross indecency with another male person, shall be guilty of a misdemeanour, and being convicted thereof shall be liable at the discretion of the Court to be imprisoned for any term not exceeding two years, with or without hard labour."

During the passing of the Bill the clause was introduced in the House of Commons by Mr Henry Labouchère, Member of Parliament for Northampton, educated at Eton and Trinity College, Cambridge, who had served in the Diplomatic Corps from 1854 to 1868 before becoming a Liberal Member of Parliament from 1865 to 1868 and again from 1880 to 1906. He cherished his reputation as a radical journalist. In 1876 he became the founder editor and owner of the weekly journal *Truth* which sought to expose sham and corruption.[1] During his lecture tour of the United States of America in 1882, Oscar Wilde asked whether anyone present read *Truth* and then said that "Labouchère is the best writer in Europe, a most remarkable gentleman".[2] Hindsight might have elicited a very different comment.

Clause 11, later to become Section 11, was inserted into the Bill without almost any and certainly no adequate consideration by Parliament of its substance. The Bill had been discussed in general at length for several days in the House of Commons and Mr Labouchère had taken an active part in the debate. On August 6, 1885, he rose to put the clause upon the paper. Another member of the House, Mr Warton, on a point of order, wished to ask whether

---

1. *Chambers Biographical Dictionary*. Magnus Magnusson. Chambers 1990.
2. *The Stranger Wilde*. Gary Schmidgall. Dutton. 1994, p.215.

the clause about to be moved, and which dealt with a totally different class of offence to that upon which the Bill was directed, was within the scope of the Bill. The Speaker rules that "At this stage of the Bill anything can be introduced into it by leave of the House."[3]

Mr Labouchère then moved his amendment which would, he said, make the law applicable to any person whether over or under the age of 13. He did not think it necessary to discuss the proposal at any length, as he understood Her Majesty's Government was willing to accept it. He therefore left it for the House and the Government to deal with as might be thought best. Thereupon and without more ado a new Clause 11 "Outrages on Public Decency" was brought up and read the first and second time.[4]

Two other members spoke. Mr Hopwood who had spoken in the general debate a large number of times said that he did not wish to say anything against the clause. However he wanted to point out that under the law as it stood, the kind of offence indicated could not be an offence in the case of any person above the age of 13 and in the case of any person under 13 there could be no consent. Sir Henry James said the clause proposed to restrict the punishment for the offence to one year's punishment, with or without hard labour. He would move to amend the clause by increasing the imprisonment to two years. Mr Labouchère had no objection to the amendment and the clause, as amended, was agreed to and added to the Bill.[5] The House then continued its debate on the other clauses of the Bill, without any further mention of Mr Labouchère's amendment.

The House of Lords considered the House of Commons' amendments on August 10, 1885, full of congratulations for themselves and the members of the other House upon the course pursued in reference to the measures contained in the Bill. The Bishop of Winchester said that whatever faults might be in the Bill, it was calculated to do a great deal of good and it would be a great

---

3. *Hansard's Parliamentary Debates.* 3rd Series. Vol.300, p.1397.
4. *Ibid.*
5. *Ibid.*, p.1398.

blessing to the country.[6] The Commons' amendments were considered and agreed on the same day. No mention at all was made of Clause 11 by any speaker in the House of Lords.

Thus it was that although buggery and attempted buggery had for over three hundred years been criminal offences whether in public or private, and whether by consenting parties or not, acts of gross indecency between consenting adults first became a criminal offence by Section 11 of the Criminal Law Amendment Act 1885. After the Royal Assent was given and the Act published, some commentators in the press and on speakers' platforms expressed their views on the Session which "certainly went much wider than Mr Labouchère's apparent intention, and it seems probable that Parliament let it pass without the detailed consideration that such an amendment would almost certainly receive today."[7] However, that may be, the amendment became and remained law for 80 years.

---

6. *Ibid.*, p.1551.
7. Report of the Committee on Homosexual Offences and Prostitution 1957. Cmnd. 247, para.108.

CHAPTER 6

Steps Towards Reform in the Nineteen-Fifties

The law forbidding gross indecency between consenting males was still the same when the Committee on Homosexual Offences and Prostitution was appointed in August 1954 under the chairmanship of Sir John Wolfenden CBE. The Committee's terms of reference were to consider, *inter alia*, the law and practice relating to homosexual offences and the treatment of persons convicted of such offences by the courts, and to report what changes, if any, were in the opinion of the Committee desirable.[1]

Before the setting-up of the Committee, two significant events had occurred. One was the publication by the Church of England of a pamphlet about homosexuality. The other was the sensational trial of Lord Montagu, Michael Pitt-Rivers and Peter Wildeblood.

The Church of England Speaks Out

In 1953 a group of Anglican clergy and doctors issued a report entitled "The Problem of Homosexuality". Although an Interim Report and for private circulation only, it had a considerate impact. Dealing with the law and the male homosexual the report emphasized the opportunity for blackmail which the prevailing law afforded:

"The young 'tout' or male prostitute offers himself for money

---

1. Report of the Committee on Homosexual Offences and Prostitution 1957. Cmnd. 247. Chairman: Sir John Wolfenden, CBE.

and being already a vicious person is able to threaten his companion with a report to the police that he has been seduced. A strong-minded man so threatened would himself go to the police but a homosexual may be so conditioned to fear the police (perhaps over a number of years) that the last thing he is ready to do is to draw the attention of the police upon himself."[2]

The Report continues:

"We have reasons to believe that inexperienced boys are in some cases seduced by the older homosexual because the latter is afraid of becoming involved with a fellow-adult who might turn and blackmail him. The continuance of the present law may well be the direct cause of harm to children who are sought out as less likely to think of blackmail and whose pledge of secrecy can be often bought or extorted under threats. If so, the law is endangering the young, not protecting them."[3]

In conclusion the Report expressed the hope that such facts as were elicited in their study of homosexuality would be regarded as of sufficient importance to deserve a full official inquiry.

The Montagu Case

In 1954, Lord Montague of Beaulieu, Michael Pitt-Rivers and Peter Wildeblood were charged with committing homosexual acts and conspiring to incite their committal.

Two younger consenting adults, Edward McNally and John Reynolds, gave evidence at the trial thereby obtaining immunity from prosecution. At Winchester Assizes, McNally and Reynolds were introduced by the prosecution as "men of the lowest possible

---

2. The Problem of Homosexuality. An Interim Report by a group of Anglican clergy and doctors (for private circulation). The Church of England Moral Welfare Council, 1953, p.21.

3. *Ibid.*, p.22(c).

moral character. Men who were corrupted, who cheerfully accepted corruption long before they met these defendants ... They are witnesses ... known as accomplices."

At the trial, letters including some of which had passed between Wildeblood and McNally, were also part of the prosecution case. On conviction Wildeblood and Pitt-Rivers were sent to prison for 18 months, Montague for 12 months.

Much sympathy was expressed in the national newspapers for the three defendants - (Wildeblood was himself a journalist) and headlines such as "Law and Hypocrisy" appeared. The newspaper articles were not complaining of the conduct of the trial, but of the fact that the law was not in accord with a large mass of public opinion. Shortly afterwards, the Wolfenden Committee was set up.

Incidentally, Peter Wildeblood paid tribute to Lord Longford who visited him every three weeks in prison whilst preparing a report for the Nuffield Foundation on the causes of crime. "Sitting with him there in a room without a warder, in a dingy grey suit which I had worn for six months, with my hands scarred by the mailbag needle and my fingernails black with ingrained dirt, I could feel that I was still a person. I can never repay him for what he did for me during those months."[4]

After his release from prison, Wildeblood wrote of his experiences in *Against the Law* and described his arrest, trial and imprisonment and return to freedom. He took a dignified open stance and made no excuse for his proclivities. He stated that he did not want to make excuses or to make denials in the fashion of Oscar Wilde. When he died in November 1999, his obituary in *The Times* of November 10, 1999, praised the book for its honesty and restraint. It also asserted that this was probably the first book on homosexuality to reach a mass audience in Britain.

Wildeblood elected to give evidence to the Wolfenden Committee. This was the first time that a homosexual had been called to represent himself publicly in front of an official inquiry. Wildeblood explained:

---

4. Peter Wildeblood. *Against the Law* Weidenfeld and Nicholson. 1955.

"It was easy for me to speak for the homosexuals because my admission that I was one of them had received the most widespread publicity; I had nothing further to lose."[5]

Report of the Wolfenden Committee

In 1957, when the Wolfenden Committee reported, the law dealing with much of the matter under review had been consolidated in the Sexual Offences Act 1956. It was still an offence for a male person to:

(a)   commit an act of gross indecency with another male person whether in public or private; or

(b)   to be party to the commission of such an act; or

(c)   to procure the commission of such an act.

"Gross indecency" was not defined by statute but it appeared to cover any act involving sexual indecency between two male persons. If two male persons were acting in concert and behaved in an indecent manner the offence was committed even though there had been no actual physical contact. In *R. v. Hunt* [1950] 34 Crim. AR 135 the appellants were found by the police making indecent exhibitions of each other though there was no physical contact between them. On appeal, Lord Goddard, LCJ, said: "I do not propose to go through the disgusting evidence in this case ... they were found in a shed in positions in which they were making filthy exhibitions the one to the other. After direction by the Deputy Chairman of Quarter Sessions that it was not necessary that there should be actual contact, they were found guilty, and this decision is upheld on appeal."

---

5. *Ibid.*, p.174. For a fuller account of Wildeblood's evidence to the Committee as well as a fascinating detailed analysis of the sociological and cultural setting to the Committee, see Professor Frank Mort's article "Mapping Sexual London: The Wolfenden Committee on Homosexual Offences and Prostitution 1954-1957". *Sexual Geographies.* Number 37, Spring 1999. Lawrence and Wishart, p.92.

Criticism was made by witnesses to the Wolfenden Committee that the Labouchère amendment, in the Criminal Law Amendment Act 1885, was frequently referred to as "the Blackmailer's Charter". The Committee took the view that the amendment certainly provided greater opportunities for the blackmailer; nevertheless:

"the fact that buggery, attempted buggery and indecent assault were already criminal offences offered ample scope for the blackmailer and would have continued to do so even if the amendment had not been passed into law. Indeed, English law has recognised the special danger of blackmail in relation to buggery and attempted buggery in Section 29 of the Larceny Act 1916."[6]

The Report of the Committee continues:

"We know that blackmail takes place in connection with homosexual acts. There is no doubt also that a good many instances occur where from fear of exposure men lay themselves open to repeated small demands for money or other benefits, which their previous conduct makes it difficult for them to resist; these often do not amount to blackmail in the strict sense, but they arise out of the same situation as gives rise to blackmail itself. Most victims of the blackmail are naturally hesitant about reporting."[7]

The Committee's Approach to the Problem

In the preface to their Report, the Committee expressed the view that where an individual's behaviour does not harm another this is a realm which is, in brief and crude terms, not the law's business. The Committee asked the question: What acts ought to be punished

---

6. The Wolfenden Committee Report, para.109.
7. *Ibid.*, para.110.

by the State?[8] In answering their own question, they said that the function of the criminal law was:

"To preserve public order and decency, to protect citizens from what is offensive or injurious, and to provide sufficient safeguards against exploitation and corruption of others, particularly those who are specially vulnerable ... It is not, in our view, the function of the law to intervene in the private lives of citizens, or to seek to enforce any particular pattern of behaviour further than is necessary to carry out the purposes we have outlined."[9]

The Wolfenden Committee robustly recommended that homosexual behaviour between consenting adults (ie, over the age of 21) in private should no longer be a criminal offence. So far as "in private" is concerned, it would be for the courts to decide, in case of doubt, whether or not public decency had been outraged. At the time in other fields of behaviour the law recognised the age of 21 as being appropriate for binding decisions to be made, eg, entering legal contracts, including the contract of marriage.

Following the Wolfenden Committee's Report all that remained was for the recommendation to abolish the offence under Section 11 of the Criminal Law Amendment Act 1885 to be incorporated into statutory form. That, however, had to wait upon the political will of the government, and it was not immediately forthcoming.

Efforts to Reform

The Homosexual Law Reform Society was founded in 1958 (Director: Antony Gray). Its first public meeting was at Caxton Hall, Westminster in May 1960. The Society had made a deliberate decision to direct its primary work at progressive public opinion rather than at the homosexual community. Essentially, the Society

---

8. *Ibid.*, para.13.
9. *Ibid.*, para.14.

was a classical middle class single-issue pressure group of a type which flourished in the 1960s.[10] One of the authors of this book vividly recalls the respect in which the Homosexual Law Reform Society was held by other would-be reformers. During the years 1958-1966, it kept up pressure, publishing leaflets, and interesting liberal members of the public in its endeavours, thus creating a climate of public opinion in which it was possible for the law to be changed in 1967.

One of the professional bodies which gave written and oral evidence to the Wolfenden Committee was the Society of Labour Lawyers. The witnesses on behalf of the Society were Mr Gerald Gardiner, QC, Mr C.R. Hewitt, Mr Ben Hooberman, Mr P.R. Kimber and Miss Jean Graham Hall. The Society had strongly campaigned for a change in both the laws of homosexuality and prostitution, in the latter case without success. The result of the effort to change the law regarding homosexual acts between consenting male adults was quite another matter.

The Society had targeted a number of areas in which it wanted to see changes, including the machinery of law reform itself, through the setting up of a Law Commission. In 1963 in a book entitled *Law Reform Now* edited by Gerald Gardiner (former chairman of the General Council of the Bar and later to become Lord Chancellor in a Labour Government) and Andrew Martin (later to become a Law Commissioner) the Society set out its stall with regard to the various law reforms which it hoped to see carried out by the next Labour government.[11]

The chapter on Criminal Law was written by C.H. Rolph, a former Chief Inspector of the City of London Police and a member of the Executive Committee of the Howard League for Penal Reform. One of the issues he dealt with was homosexuality:

"It is curious that lesbianism or homosexuality between women is no offence whilst sexual relations between men or between

---

10. Jeffery Weeks. *Coming Out*. Quartet Books. 1977, p.168 and p.171.
11. *Law Reform Now*. Ed: Gerald Gardiner, QC, and Andrew Martin, PhD, Gollancz, 1963.

men and animals can be punished by imprisonment for life (maximum sentence). This law appears to be based entirely on prejudice and bigotry and no estimate is made of any actual injury to the community which may have been caused by the offence ... if the crime is analysed it must be seen that, apart from elements of cruelty to children or animals or a nuisance if it is committed in a public place or place of public resort, little or no direct injury to the community is entailed ... The moderate recommendations of the Wolfenden Committee, removing private homosexual acts between males from the area of criminal law (as in the case of females) should be put into effect without further delay. The delay hitherto has been inexplicable."[12]

Other bodies and organisations may have given up hope of any reform - but never one led by Gerald Gardiner. He always reminded his fellow would-be reformers that on average one had to wait 21 years from the date of a Government Committee's Report to the implementations of its recommendations. There was a reduction in this instance to 10 years. Through his influence many reforms were passed and in the opinion of the authors - one of whom knew him well - (being the Secretary of the Society of Labour Lawyers for 11 years) he is rightly remembered as a great, modest and reforming Lord Chancellor.

---

12. *Ibid.*, p.244.

CHAPTER 7

The Abolition of Section Eleven - A Long Haul

The short answer to the question "Could Oscar Wilde or any other person committing the same acts which the second jury found proved in 1885 be charged with a criminal offence today?" is "No".

Although by the time the Wolfenden Committee completed its Report in 1957 the Sexual Offences Act 1956 had reiterated the position of the Criminal Law Offences Act 1895, Section 11, nothing further occurred until the passing of the Sexual Offenders Act 1967.

By Section 1 of the Sexual Offenders Act 1967:

(1)   Notwithstanding any statutory or common law provision, a homosexual act in private shall not be an offence provided that the parties consent thereto and have attained the age of 21 years.

(2)   Any act which would otherwise be treated for the purpose of this Act as being done in private shall not be treated if done -

(a)   when more than two persons take part or are present; or

(b)   in a lavatory to which the public have or are permitted to have access whether on payment or otherwise.

The *Criminal Justice and Public Order Act 1994,* Section 145(1) reduces the age of consenting men in private from 21 to 18. Section 146(1) extended this to the armed forces and the merchant navy.

However, there remained some restrictions. By Section 146(4):

"Nothing contained in this section shall prevent a homosexual act, with or without other acts or circumstances, from constituting a ground for discharging a member of HM armed forces from the service or dismissing a member of the crew of a UK merchant ship from his ship, or in the case of a member of HM armed forces when the act occurs in conjunction with other acts or circumstances from constituting an offence under the Army Act 1995 or the Navy Discipline Act 1957."

Attempt at a "Labouchère Amendment" in 1998

An attempt was made to introduce a new clause in the Crime and Disorder Bill (Lords) on June 22, 1998. The House of Commons was debating the Lords Bill, to reduce the age at which certain sexual acts are lawful and to substitute 16 for 18 years of age in Section 1(a) and 1(c) of Section 12 of the Sexual Offences Act 1956 which deals with buggery, and in Section 13 dealing with gross indecency.

In moving the new clause, Ann Keen, MP, said that this debate was about equality. The purpose was to make the age of consent equal to everyone. "We are one of the last nations in the European Union yet to legislate for equality on the age of consent. Just over a week ago the Finnish Parliament passed a similar law, on an unanimous vote, without one speaker opposing it."[1] The Bill was read a third time as amended and passed by the House of Commons. It went back to the House of Lords which rejected the amendment. A game of ping-pong then ensued between the two Houses. As the Bill originated in the House of Lords, the Lords had the power to reject any amendments on the Bill, which in the main contained important provisions dealing with crime and disorder generally. The Government wanted those main provisions passed into law before the summer recess, and therefore persuaded a sufficient number in the House of Commons not to try to move the new clause again. The age of consent for consenting males taking part in homosexual acts in private therefore remained at 18 years.

---

1. *Hansard HC.* 1998. Vol.314. Col.756.

It is interesting to note that the mover of the amendment, Ann Keen, tried to do what Henry Labouchère had succeeded in doing in the House of Commons in 1885 - ie, insert a clause into a Bill, the main provisions of which dealt with entirely different matters. This time, however, the Government realised what was happening and promised that the matter would be given more time, in a separate House of Commons Bill, in the near future.

The Queen's Speech November 1998

In the Queen's Speech of November 1998 the Government announced that it would introduce an Age of Consent Bill in the forthcoming Parliamentary Session. The age of consent between consenting homosexual males for acts committed in private would be lowered to 16 years of age. The Bill would include safeguards to protect youths aged 16 and 17 from those in authority, eg, teachers at school and social workers responsible for young people in care. The Bill would be on a free vote. This time the Bill would commence in the House of Commons, to minimise the effect of any constitutional clash with the House of Lords.

A few weeks later the Government explained their proposals for the Bill. A new criminal offence, ie, "abuse of trust" would be created, which would apply to adults such as teachers, social workers and others who have authority over young people. The clause would not cover the armed forces. The Home Office intended to draw up a national register conscripting anyone believed to impose a threat to young people, to ensure that any of them who are vulnerable will be protected from abuse. In England, Scotland and Wales the reduction of the age for homosexual consent will be lowered to 16 years. In Northern Ireland, where the age of homosexual consent is 17, that age will also apply to homosexual consent.

Some are Still More Equal than Others

During the debate in the House of Commons on the Crime and

Disorders Bill in June 1998 the Minister of State at the Home Office, Mr Alan Michael, announced that there would be a comprehensive review of the current legislation and penalties for several offences, eg, sex between males is still unlawful, even if it takes place in private, between consenting adults if more than two people are present [Sexual Offences Act 1967 Section 1[2]]. No such restriction exists on heterosexual sex.

The Review commenced in February 1999 with the following terms of reference "to review the sex offence in statute and common law in England and Wales and to make recommendations that will:

(i)   provide coherent and clear sexual offences which protect the individual, particularly the most vulnerable, from abuse and exploitation;
(ii)   enable abusers to be appropriately punished;
(iii)   be fair and non-discriminating in accordance with the ECHR and Human Rights Act."

The Review was expected to last about a year and to produce proposals which could then form the basis of a public consultation.[3] Hopes were expressed that draft legislation could be ready for inclusion in the Queen's Speech in November 2000.[4] That would coincide with the anniversary of Oscar Wilde's death exactly one hundred years earlier.

Keeping to its promise, the Government introduced the new Bill on January 25, 1999. The Secretary of State for the Home Department, Mr Jack Straw, explained that the new Bill fell into two quite separate parts, both applying to the United Kingdom as a whole.

The first, in Clause 1, is the issue of the age of consent for male homosexuals. The second separate issue is abuse of trust. That arises from widely shared concerns about the need to protect vulnerable

---

2. *Ibid.* 1999. Vol.324. Col.20.
3. Martin Bowley, QC. "An Overdue Reform". *New Law Journal*. Butterworths. January 1999, p.141.
4. *Ibid.*

young people. "We are dealing with the matter in the Bill because of the very strong views about the vulnerability of 16 and 17 year olds of both Houses last summer." Mr Straw pointed out that in 1997 there were two cautions, nine prosecutions and seven convictions of those aged 18 and over for buggery with 16 and 17 year olds.[5]

The Relationship of Trust set out in the Bill

1. Young persons in any form of detention.
2. Those looked after by local authorities, in a children's home, in foster care or in semi-independent accommodation.
3. Those resident in an institution providing health or social care, a hospital, a children's home, a nursing home or other forms of residential care.
4. Area of full-time education. The Minister of State, Mr Paul Boateng, said that here the teacher stands in *loco parentis.*

On introducing the Bill in the House of Lords on April 13, 1999, Lord Williams of Mostyn, the Minister of State, Home Office, reminded the House that as a matter of duty we should ensure equality before the criminal law for young homosexuals and heterosexuals:

"This concerns a fundamental principle of equality and the Bill would bring that about ... We are not advocating sexual promiscuity. We are not opening up floodgates of social change for further reductions in the age of consent ... The age of 16 is about right. The proposals here, if one approaches it in the dual way I commend is simply to bear in mind that the age of consent for heterosexual relationships is set at 16 ... it has been with us for a long time."[6]

Lord Williams gave a long list of organisations which support the

5. *Hansard HC.* 1999. Vol.324. Col.20.
6. *Hansard HL.* 1999. Vol.324. Col.648.

equalisation of the age of consent, and reminded the House that those organisations do not consist of revolutionaries and are not subversive of normal order. He then dealt with the abuse of trust proposed which governs both heterosexual and homosexual relationships, as they should, and are part of a wider programme for protecting children and the vulnerable.[7]

Lord Williams assured the House that no legislation of homosexual marriage would be proposed by the Government, and that there would be no legal adoption by homosexual couples.

The Lords debated at some length, during which time Earl Russell said, "This Bill will become law. The only question is whether it becomes law this year or the next year; not sometime or never, but only this year or next year." However, the majority of peers voted against, and the Bill was lost.

Fair Play for Homosexuals in the Armed Forces

The cases of *Lustig-Prean and Becket v. United Kingdom* and *Smith and Grady v. United Kingdom* before the European Court of Human Rights (*The Times*, October 11, 1999) constitute an important victory for homosexuals in the Armed Forces. The four applicants were all at the relevant time members of the Forces. Each applicant, one of whom was a woman, admitted their homosexuality under rigorous investigation by the service police. Their activities were off-base and in private. Each applicant was administratively discharged on the sole ground of their sexual orientation. Having exhausted all their domestic remedies, they lodged their applications with the European Court of Human Rights.

The court held that there was a breach of the European Convention on Human Rights in that the investigations conducted into the applicants' sexual orientation together with their discharge constituted especially grave interference with their private lives and were unjustified. The court was not persuaded by the UK Government's argument that medical security and disciplinary

---

7. *Ibid.*, col.649.

reasons necessitated the investigations.

Within a few days of the judgment of the court the newly appointed Defence Secretary, Geoff Hoon, made an announcement promising a new policy, in accordance with the judgment, would be implemented as quickly as possible.

The decision of the European Court of Human Rights has been generally welcomed as a victory for reason over pure prejudice. Writing in *The Times* in October 1999, David Pannick, QC, stated:

"The judgment had important implications for the application of human rights law in this country. Each of the applicants served with distinction until the Ministry of Defence investigated, and acted on, their sexual orientation even though it had hitherto remained private and off-base. The European Court accepted that there was no evidence that homosexuality caused any practical problems for the Armed Forces far less any difficulties which could not properly be addressed by a code of discipline that focused on conduct rather than penalising an aspect of private personality."

The Defence Secretary, Mr Geoffrey Hoon, immediately announced that a new policy would be implemented after consultations with the defence chiefs to conform to international law. In the House of Commons in January 2000 he said that there would be no requirement for anyone to disclose his or her sexual orientation either at the recruitment stage or during service in the Forces.

A Final Comment

We would not claim that some legal restrictions do not remain against same-sex relationships. The walls of Jericho have, however, been widely breached, even if they have not yet completely disappeared.

How different from 105 years ago! However, if Wilde had led a more circumspect existence with Bosie, and with the rent boys on whom he spent so lavishly, it is likely that, although in breach of the criminal law, his style of life would not have led to prosecution. It was only through his own deliberate decision to bring a prosecution against the Marquess of Queensberry for criminal libel that the inevitable and devastating chain of events started, and progressed to its tortuous end. Over 100 years on, it would all have been so different. Provided he continued to conduct his sexual life in private, he would have been permitted to do so by laws of a much more liberal and understanding society.

CHAPTER 8

Costs Incurred in the Trials

A Journey to Carey Street for Bankruptcy Proceedings

The bankruptcy proceedings, a civil process, were instigated in June 1895 by solicitors for the Marquess of Queensberry filing a petition in the Bankruptcy Court in Carey Street. The sum claimed against Wilde was £677, being the amount of the petitioner's taxed costs in the criminal libel suit brought unsuccessfully against him by Wilde. The proceedings were perfectly legal and the Marquess even with his intense dislike of Wilde, had every right to bring them.

It has been categorically stated that at the trial Wilde had "received definite assurances from Lord Alfred Douglas that the various members of the Queensberry family who hated its titular head, particularly Douglas's elder brother Lord Douglas of Hawick, would be responsible for the cost of the libel prosecution into which Alfred Douglas had vigorously egged Wilde on."[1] This does not accord with Bosie's own account in which he says:

"It has been widely asserted that I went out of my way to instigate these proceedings against my father - It is quite certain that I did not go on my bended knees to ask Wilde not to take proceedings. He assured me that the suggestions and accusations against him were quite false and without foundation. I had not the smallest reason to suppose that he was lying to me, and I undoubtedly allowed matters to take their course ... On the morning the warrant was executed Wilde came to me in a condition bordering on hysteria, told me that he had no money and that at least £300 was required in order that the case might

---

1. H. Montgomery Hyde. *Oscar Wilde - a Biography*. Eyre Methuen. 1976, p.224.

BITER

THE ARREST OF OSCAR WILDE
Illustrated Police Budget, 335
April 13, 1895, 335
By permission of The British Library

BIT!!

PROSECUTOR AND PRISONER CHANGE PLACES

Letter from Oscar Wilde to his wife Constance
Courtesy of Magdalen College Oxford MS 399
Written circa 1895. Dated to February 1895,
just before the Criminal Libel Trial

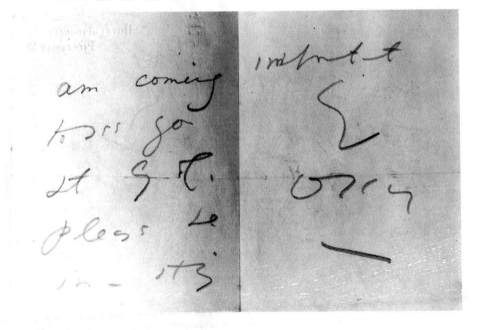

Oscar Wilde
16 October 1854 - 30 November 1900

Père Lachaise Cemetery, Paris
Oscar Wilde's final resting place

photograph by April Knutson

go on. At his urgent solicitation I gave him £300 to give to his solicitor ... Wilde for his part pointed out that it was entirely through his friendship for me that he had to suffer Lord Queensberry's insults, and that unless he went on with the prosecution he would be branded throughout Europe as a person of a vicious and abominable life, and that, as I had been the means of getting him into trouble, it would be a poor thing if I would not find a few hundred to get him out again. What was I to do - and what would any man so placed have done?"[2]

The Oscar Wilde Society includes amongst its members a number with encyclopaedic knowledge of the writer. Currently opinion is sharply divided as to Bosie's part in Oscar's tragedy. Certainly in *De Profundis*, addressed to Bosie from HM Prison, Reading, and written over a period January-March 1897, Wilde himself was explicit as to Bosie's involvement:

"I felt most strongly, and still feel, and will revert to the subject again, that these costs should have been paid up by your family. You had taken personally on yourself the responsibility of stating that your family would do so. It was that which had made the solicitor take up the case in the way he did. You were absolutely responsible."

Wilde goes on to explain:

"When I told the solicitor I had no money to face the gigantic expense, you interposed at once. You said that your own family would be only too delighted to pay all the necessary costs: that your father had been an incubus to them all: that they had often discussed the possibility of getting him put into a lunatic asylum so as to keep him out of the way: that he was a daily source of annoyance and distress to your mother and everyone else: that if I would only come forward to have him shut up I would be regarded by the family as their champion and their benefactor

---

2. Lord Alfred Douglas. *Oscar Wilde and Myself*. John Long. 1914, p.94.

and that your mother's rich relations would regard it as a great delight to be allowed to pay all costs and expenses that might be incurred in any such effort. The solicitor closed at once, and I was hurried to the Police Court. I had no excuse left for not going. I was forced into it."

In any event, while he was serving time in prison for criminal offences of gross indecency Wilde was taken to Carey Street, Chancery Lane, London, for the bankruptcy proceedings, and in *De Profundis* described his humiliation mitigated only by the loving gesture of Robbie Ross:

> "When I was brought down from my prison to the Court of Bankruptcy between two policemen, Robbie waited in the long dreary corridor that, before the whole crowd, whom an action so sweet and simple hushed into silence, he might gravely raise his hat to me, as with lowered head I passed him by. Men have gone to heaven *for sweeter things* than that."[3]

Wilde continued to complain bitterly about Bosie's conduct and its dire consequences, ie, that the law had taken from him not merely all that he had - books, furniture, pictures, copyright in plays, but also all that he was ever going to have, ie:

> "My interest in my marriage settlement for instance was sold. Fortunately I was able to buy it in, through friends. Otherwise in case my wife died, my two children during my lifetime would be as penniless as myself. My interest in our Irish estate, entailed on me by my own father, will I suppose have to go next."

It was not until 1906, six years after Wilde's death that Robbie Ross, was able to announce that all Wilde's creditors had been paid in full.

The Insolvency Act 1985 replaced the earlier Bankruptcy Act and produced a new and simplified code. Basically, however, the procedure today would be the same as it was in 1895. There is some

---

3. *De Profundis*. Harper Collins. 1994, p.1011.

change concerning assets in bankruptcy, but that would have made little difference to Wilde today. Imprisonment for bankruptcy had generally been abolished by the Debtors Act 1878, and it was only fortuitous that Wilde was serving a period of imprisonment for criminal offences when the petition against him was served.

By the Insolvency Act 1985, Section 264, a petition for a bankruptcy order to be made against an individual may be presented to the court by, *inter alia,* one of the individual's creditors, in the same fashion as the Marquess of Queensberry. A debtor's petition may be presented to the court only on the ground that the debtor is unable to pay his debts. An application for an order of the court discharging an individual from bankruptcy may be made at any time after the end of the period beginning with the commencement of the bankruptcy.

A Generous Gesture to an Impecunious Client

Throughout the whole of *De Profundis,* in which Wilde returns several times to complain at length against the costs which he must pay to the Marquess of Queensberry, he makes no mention at all of the generosity of Sir Edward Clarke and his colleagues who appeared, without fee, for Wilde as prosecutors in that trial, and also for Wilde as a defendant in the two trials which followed.

When the Marquess of Queensberry left his obnoxious visiting card at the Albermarle Club, Oscar Wilde consulted the solicitors recommended by Robert Ross, Messrs C.O. Humphreys, Son and Kershaw, a firm of unassailable integrity. Travers Humphreys, a relative of the senior partner, who had a complementary junior brief for Wilde, explained that Wilde's solicitor had not the faintest idea that Wilde had laid himself open to charges such as those upon which he was ultimately convicted:

"In giving to his solicitor, as he afterwards admitted, his solemn assurance of his innocence, Wilde lied, as did Lord Alfred Douglas who accompanied him. None of Wilde's friends came forward to give the solicitors even the hint of the life Wilde had been leading, though they were ready enough at a later stage to offer information upon it."[4]

At the committal proceedings in the Great Marlborough Street Magistrates Court the Marquess of Queensberry was represented by Mr E.H. Carson, QC, MP and Mr C.F. Gill. The next Old Bailey Sessions were due to open in less than three weeks' time and Mr C.O. Humphreys was determined to obtain the best possible legal representation for Wilde. Accordingly he offered the brief to Sir Edward Clarke, QC, MP, a former Solicitor General. Clarke had never met Wilde before he was instructed in this case and he requested a meeting with him, and the next day Mr C.O. Humphreys took Wilde to Sir Edward's chambers in the Temple.

"I can only accept this brief, Mr Wilde," said Clarke, "if you can assure me on your honour as an English gentleman that there is not and never has been any foundation for the charges that are made against you."[5]

Wilde declared on his honour that the charges were absolutely false and groundless. Wilde was technically the prosecutor in the criminal libel case, Clarke was therefore perfectly entitled to ask for this assurance. If Wilde had been the defendant Clarke would not have done so. It would have been contrary to the professional etiquette and tradition of the Bar for counsel to make his client's declaration of innocence a condition of defending him.

Sir Edward Clarke realised that he was being asked to act for an impecunious client, and he therefore offered to appear without a fee. The same applied to his juniors, Mr C.W. Matthews and Mr Travers Humphreys. These magnanimous gestures were not universally appreciated at the time, nor the dire financial circumstances of the client.

At the conclusion of the criminal libel case against the Marquess

---

4. H. Montgomery Hyde. Ed. Notable British Trials. *The Trial of Oscar Wilde.* Foreword - the Rt. Hon. Sir Travers Humphreys PC. William Hodge. 1948, p.3.
5. H. Montgomery Hyde. *Oscar Wilde - a Biography.* Eyre Methuen. 1976, p.203.

of Queensberry, Wilde himself was indicted to stand trial. Sir Edward Clarke once again offered his services as counsel, without a fee. If he or some other member of the Bar had not done so, it is difficult to see how Wilde could have been legally represented at the two trials which followed.

At the time of the trial, the *Law Journal* did not appreciate the kindness and generosity of the ex-Solicitor General, nor the financial position of the defendant:

> "Strange stories get into the newspaper. One such has come under our notice which we refuse to credit. It is stated that Sir Edward Clarke has offered to defend Mr Oscar Wilde at the Old Bailey without a fee. It is clearly contrary to the etiquette of the Bar for a counsel to defend a prisoner for less than the minimum sum recognised by old-established usage, except by request of the presiding judge. Nor is Mr Oscar Wilde a case in which such a nominal fee could properly be accepted. It has never been suggested that his circumstances are not such as to enable him to pay for his defence on the scale that counsel in the eminent position of Sir Edward Clarke is entitled to accept."
>
> *Obiter Dicta*, April 13, 1895

Six weeks later, however, the *Law Journal* was unctuous in its praise of Sir Edward's personal abilities:

> "The ludicrous suggestion which has been made in certain quarters that Sir Edward Clarke will suffer particularly by his brilliant and strenuous advocacy in the Wilde case might well be passed over in silence were it not the duty of counsel in defending prisoners in a subject on which very many people entertain hazy ideas. It is not necessary to dwell on the supreme ability and courage with which Sir Edward Clarke fought this difficult and losing battle ... The advocate may use the weapons of the soldier but not the dagger of the assassin. But the most strenuous defence is right even of the worst criminals, and is in accordance with the best interests of society as a whole."
>
> June 1, 1895

After the second criminal trial in which Wilde was a defendant *The Law Times* also paid tribute:

"The devotion of Sir Edward Clarke to the course of a client who, at his best, was a moral monstrosity, is startling. It has been called heroic. Possibly it was - had it been successful the achievement would have been phenomenal. But it failed, and the worthlessness of the cause which received a self-sacrifice of every kind becomes painfully prominent. The Bar is supposed by the public to be a blood-sucking profession. How often its members work for nothing the public know not. Few barristers are grasping builders of fortunes. Very many vehemently support causes in which they have once embarked with absolute self-abandonment. Conspicuous instances may bring this home to the popular mind."

> *Law Times.* "Law and the Lawyers". Vol.99, June 1, 1895

The article in *The Law Times* went on to acknowledge that the ex-Solicitor-General was fighting an uphill fight - leading with a hope, if not forlorn, yet desperate. In the third trial, the Solicitor-General, Sir Frank Lockwood, QC, appearing for the prosecution, had to face a fierce and watchful defence - and "get rid of that dangerous glamour of 'art' which Wilde himself imprudently attempted to throw over the filthiness of his crimes, and which his advocate courageously supported by eloquence of which the theme was wholly unworthy."

For anyone facing serious criminal charges today the situation could not be more different. There would be no need to rely on unpaid representation by a successor of Sir Edward Clarke. The Legal Aid and Advice Act 1949 followed the recommendations of a committee set up by the Lord Chancellor in 1945 under the chairmanship of Lord Rushcliffe. The Rushcliffe Committee recommended that legal aid should be available in all courts, both criminal and civil. The Committee also recommended that the legal aid should not be limited to those normally classed as poor, but should include a wider income group. Barristers and solicitors would receive adequate remuneration, from public funds. Under the Legal Aid Act 1988 representation is available to the accused in criminal proceedings, including any proceedings preliminary or incidental to the proceedings, including bail applications. However, by Section 21(5) representation would not be available unless it appeared to the legal aid authority that the accused's financial resources were such as to make him eligible under the Act. The decision must always be based on the information contained in the form of application for legal aid, together with any other oral or written information provided on or on behalf of applicant.

According to the National Audit Office, reporting in 1998, there has been a certain amount of inefficiency in the administration of the scheme in recent years. In 38 per cent of the cases mistakes have been made regarding the amounts of money defendants could and should contribute. Changes in the methods of administration, hopefully will result in lesser calls upon public funds under the Access to Justice Act 1999, which replaces the Legal Aid Board with the Legal Services Commission. The latter will have, *inter alia,* responsibility for maintaining and developing the Criminal Defence Service.

Today Sir Edward Clarke would be able to appear for Oscar Wilde in the trial and retrial of the criminal charges under this system, and both he and his junior would be adequately rewarded from public funds. That would not be the case, however, in the criminal libel proceedings in which Oscar Wilde was technically the prosecutor. The legal aid service is only available for defendants in criminal cases, and not private prosecutions. If the Crown Prosecution Service refused to take over the private prosecution today Oscar Wilde would either himself have to bear the cost of legal representation or once again rely on the kindness, good will and generous *pro bono* gesture of an Edward Clarke.

CHAPTER 9

The Law of Homosexuality Overseas

In the United States of America

In December 1882, at the invitation of the D'Oyly Carte New York office, Oscar Wilde sailed for New York on the *SS Arizona* and commenced what turned out to be an extensive lecture tour lasting 10 months. He enjoyed considerable hospitality and wide publicity, eventually returning to England from New York on the *SS Bothnia* at the end of October 1883. The total receipts of the tour were 18,215.86 dollars. Oscar's half-share of the profits amounted to 8,605.31 dollars. Most of his lectures were on the Decorative Arts or Aesthetics "the science of the beautiful", and were generally rated as a great success. On the voyage home he wrote:

"I fear I cannot picture America as altogether an Elysium - perhaps from the ordinary standpoint. I know but little about the country, I cannot give its latitude or longitude. I cannot compute the value of its dry goods, and I have no very close acquaintance with its politics ... America is a land of unmatched vitality and vulgarity, a people who care not at all about values other than their own, and who, when they make up their minds, love you and hate you with a passionate zeal."[1]

There are no accounts of any sexual activity by Oscar during his sojourn in the USA. However it is interesting to note that in all the States at the end of the nineteenth century the criminal law of each forbade any homosexual behaviour. It was not until 1961 that the first of them, Illinois, adopted the American Law Institute Moral

---

1. H. Montgomery Hyde. *Oscar Wilde - a Biography*. Eyre Methuen. 1976, p.81.

Penal Code provision which decriminalised adult, consensual, private, sexual conduct. The next State to follow was Connecticut in 1969. Currently 24 States and the District of Columbia impose criminal sanctions on consenting adults who engage in private homosexual intercourse.[2]

A challenge to the State law of Georgia, one of the 24, was made in 1982 in the case of *Bowers v. Hardwick*. In that year Atlanta police arrested Michael Hardwick in his own bedroom and charged him with committing sodomy with another consenting adult male. According to Georgia State statute:

"A person commits the offence of sodomy when he performs or submits to any sexual act involving sex organs of one person and the mouth or anus of another."

In the Municipal Court of Atlanta the district attorney decided not to pursue the case, presumably for lack of evidence. Hardwick, however, filed suit in the US District Court alleging that the statute was unconstitutional because it violated his right to privacy. He was joined in the suit by a married couple, using the pseudonyms John and Mary Doe. They claimed that the existence and enforcement of the statute "chilled and deterred their desire to engage in sexual activity". The district court and the court of appeals found that the Does lacked proper standing to maintain the action.[3]

The US Supreme Court in *Bowers v. Hardwick* 1986 (478 US 186 1065 Cr 284) held, by a majority of 5-4 that the statute was constitutional. Delivering a majority judgment, Chief Justice Burger said that, "decisions of individuals relating to homosexual conduct have been subject to state intervention throughout the history of Western civilisation. Condemnation of those practices is firmly rooted in Judea - Christian moral and ethical standards ... To hold that the act of homosexual sodomy is somehow protected as a fundamental right would be to cast aside millennia of moral teaching."

---

2. 40 *U Miami L.. Rev.*, p.521.
3. *Ibid.*, p.638.

In a dissenting judgment Justice Blackman said that only the most wilful blindness could obscure the fact that sexual intimacy is "a sensitive key of human relationship, central to family life, community welfare, and the development of human personality."

The contrast of approach by the courts in the USA and in Great Britain to the moral aspects of the law was highlighted by Eugene Restow, Professor at the Law School, Yale, in a review of a lecture by Lord Devlin in 1959. Writing in the shadow of the Wolfenden Report but before any change of the relevant law in either country, Professor Restow pointed out that in Great Britain the suggestion that law has a moral content seems to raise theocratic ghosts in many quarters, perhaps in most. In the United States it is the other way round. Every American schoolboy - or at least every American law student - considers the strict separation of law and morals to have certain hallmarks.[4]

Devlin asked himself those questions:

1. Has society the right to pass judgment at all on matters of morals? Ought there, in other words, to be a public morality, or are morals always a matter for private judgment?
2. If society has the right to pass judgment, has it also the right to use the weapon in all cases or only in some, and if only in some on what principles should it distinguish?[5]

Devlin believed that the State has a right to violation if the code of public morality through criminal law and society may use the law to preserve morality in the same way as it uses it to safeguard anything else that is essential. However, he is the first to assert that this general proposition does not in itself settle particular cases. All crimes may be sin in Devlin's analysis, but he does not believe that all sin should be made criminal. The two spheres are indissolubly linked but they are not and should not be co-existive. The

---

4. Professor Eugene V. Rostow. "The Enforcement of Morals". *Cambridge Law Journal.* A review of the Maccabean Lecture by Lord Justice Devlin in Jurisprudence, of the British Academy. 1959. Stevens 1960, p.174.
5. *Ibid.*

lawmakers must strike a balance, as they must in every other respect of the conflict between liberty and order.[6]

Homosexual Laws in Ireland

Oscar Fingal O'Flahertie Wills Wilde was born in Dublin on October 16, 1854. He went to the Portora Royal School, with his elder brother Willie, as a boarder from 1864 until 1871. In that year he won a scholarship to Trinity College, Dublin, and followed his brother there. He came to England in 1874 to take up a Demy-ship (scholarship) in Classics at Magdalen College, Oxford. After that date Oscar Wilde spent little time in Ireland. That may be just as well because Section 11 of the Criminal Law Amendment Act 1885, prohibiting gross indecency between adult consenting males, whether in private or public, applied to Ireland. It was not repealed until 1993.

In 1989, an Irish national and member of the Irish Parliament, as well as being a homosexual and chairman of the Irish Gay Rights Movement tested the law before the European Court of Human Rights. At no time was he charged with any offence. He instituted proceedings in the High Court of Ireland in 1977 [*Norris v. Ireland*. European Court of Human Rights 1989. Ser A No.142 13 EHRR 186] seeking a declaration that certain laws prohibiting homosexual relations were invalid under the Irish constitution. Those laws included Section 11.

The High Court of Ireland found that one of the effects of criminal sanctions against homosexual acts "is to reinforce the misapprehension and general prejudice of the public and increase the anxiety and guilt feelings of homosexuals leading, on occasion, to depression." However, the Judge dismissed the action on legal grounds, and the decision was upheld in 1983 by the Supreme Court of Ireland, which found the laws complained of to be consistent with the constitution since no right of privacy encompassing consensual homosexuality could be derived from the "Christian and democratic

---

6. *Ibid.*, p.176. Professor Rostow's Comments on Lord Devlin's Lecture.

nature of the Irish State".

Mr Norris commenced proceedings before the European Committee on Human Rights, claiming that the Irish Laws constituted a continuing interference with his right to respect for private life under Article 8 of the European Convention. The case was then referred to the European Court which held that it is no longer considered to be necessary or appropriate to treat homosexual practices of the kind now in question as in themselves a matter to which the sanctions of the criminal law should be applied; nevertheless the criminal law of Ireland was not altered; and Section II of the Criminal Law Amendment Act 1895 remained on the statute book.

Although the Director of Public Prosecutions had the legal right to do otherwise, since the Office of the Director was created in 1984 no prosecution had been brought in respect of homosexual activities except where minors were involved or the acts were committed in public or without consent.

The crimes of buggery and gross indecency between consenting adults over the age of 17 were abolished by the Criminal Law (Sexual Offences) Act 1993 - an Act (*inter alia*) to amend the law in relation to sexual offences and for that purpose to amend the offences against the Person Act 1861 in relation to buggery, and to amend the Criminal Law Amendment Acts 1885 to 1935.

Haven in France

De Profundis written by Oscar Wilde during his last months in prison was, as Robert Ross states in the preface, "the only work he wrote while in prison and the last work in prose he ever wrote."[7]

"I am to be released, if all goes well with me, towards the end of May and hope to go at once to some little seaside village abroad with Robbie and More."[8]

---

7. Oscar Wilde. *De Profundis*. Metheun 1905, 2nd Edition Preface.
8. *Ibid.*, p.145.

The country he chose was France. No doubt one of the considerations that influenced Wilde was the liberality of the laws of that country in respect of consensual sexual relations between adults of the same sex. Ever since 1791 only acts of public indecency have offended against the criminal law. Furthermore, the law in France does not distinguish between buggery and other homosexual acts committed in private between consenting males. In May 1863 the age of consent was set at 13 years. That continued until 1942 when the Vichy government raised the age of consent for homosexual (but not heterosexual) relations to 21. The Vichy regime did not however recriminalise homosexuality. Only since August 1982 has the age of consent in France been the same, ie, 15 for both heterosexual and homosexual relations.[9] Thus we see that, except during the years 1942-82, French law since 1791 has dealt with sex crimes without regard to the sex or sexual orientation of those involved.[10]

Although, unlike countries in Western Europe, French law in the nineteenth century did not ban any sexual activities between consenting adults, there was from the point of view of the police a distinct link between homosexual activities and crime, ie, same sex activities, particularly in public, could easily cause a scandal and have an impact on the life of the neighbourhood and perhaps not leading to violent crime, at least to petty crimes such as theft. Blackmail was also associated with male prostitution, which was prevalent in certain parts of Paris.[11]

Jealousy between cohabiting, consenting adults is not unknown in any country. The killing of Jean Baptiste Mourgues by Joseph Aimé Journeux is a case in point. On a night in October 1877, Paris police were alerted by Journeux, 36, an umbrella salesman, to Mourgues, struggling and ultimately drowning in the Seine. At that

---

9. Michael David Sibalis. "The Regulation of Male Homosexuality in Revolutionary and Napoleonic France, 1789-1815." *Homosexuality in Modern France*. Oxford University Press. 1996, p.84.

10. *Ibid.*, p.85.

11. William A. Penison. *Homosexuality in Modern France* (Ed) "Love and Death in Gay Paris - Homosexuality and Criminality in the 1870s." *Oxford University Press*. 1996, p.130.

stage Journeux claimed that he did not know the victim, and was only passing by.

The juge d'instruction in charge of the case discovered that in fact the two men knew one another very well. They had frequently been seen eating together in cafés and at places, eg, the Bamboulère Restaurant where homosexuals congregated. Mourgues, age 26, a jeweller, had lived at Journeux's apartment for about three months before his death. At least two witnesses had seen the men quarrelling and on at least one occasion fighting with each other. Journeux, who was known for his earlier homosexual activities, was apparently jealous of Mourgues. Journeux accused Mourgues of having affairs with other men.[12]

After the drowning and on being interrogated by the police Journeux offered several versions of what had occurred, eg, suicide, after a quarrel between them at the Chateau Rouge. However, the medical evidence at the trial indicated that Mourgues's body had marks on it, particularly round the neck, indicating a struggle. Mourgues's body also had the physical signs of a possible sodomite, ie, an abscess on his anus. Evidence had been given of his earlier homosexual habits but Journeux denied these probably in the belief that the jury might have interpreted them as an admission that he was guilty of murder. In the absence of evidence of predetermination, the jury found him guilty of manslaughter.

William A. Penison, writing at some length on the trial comments that Journeux was probably responsible for Mourgues's death, which he caused in a fit of rage, but in many ways, he was as much on trial for his sexual habits as for his actions on the night of the murder.[13]

Other European Countries

The age of consent has been 15 in Greece since 1987; in Belgium, Germany and Italy the age of consent is 16.

---

12. *Ibid.*, p.128/9.
13. *Ibid.*, p.141.

The Queen's Speech in November 1999 reiterated the government's promise to bring in legislation to lower the age of consent to 16 for homosexual relations. Earlier in January 1999, speaking in the House of Commons in favour of reducing the age of consent for male homosexuals to 16 years on the grounds of equality before the law, Mr Jack Straw, the Home Secretary reminded the House that the age of consent for heterosexuals was 16 in this country. He went on to say:

"The age of consent varies greatly from one European country to another (12 in Spain to 18 in Luxembourg). I see no evidence that the equal age of consent has caused any problems in any of these countries, but it must be said that the age that has been established, which ranges over that wide span of six years often reflects considerable differences in history and family traditions. In those other European countries there are often norms which ensure that the kinds of conduct about which people would be extremely anxious do not on the whole take place. It must be said that where the age of consent is lower than 16 there are often powerful offences in respect of those, say over 18s who seek to have sexual influence with those under the age of 16."[14]

---

14. *Hansard HC.* 1999. Vol.324. Col.20.

CHAPTER 10

Legal Miscellany

Evidence in Conspiracy Cases

A contemporary issue of *The Law Journal* (*infra*) raised the point that in the first trial, *R. v. Wilde and Taylor*, the defendants were charged together in the same indictment with offences against the Criminal Law Amendment Act 1885, Section 11, and also conspiracy to commit such offences. By Section 20 of the Act the accused were competent but not compellable witnesses in respect of offences created by the Act. However, this right to give evidence did not extend to a charge of conspiracy, which was a common law offence.

Sir Edward Clarke for Wilde and Mr J.R. Grain for Taylor raised objections to the indictment as a preliminary issue on the grounds that counts to which different rules applied could not be tried together and could not be legally joined. Mr Justice Charles declined to adopt either course.

The Law Journal commented:

"The fact that a defendant can give evidence on one count but not on another determines nothing as to the common law right to join the counts, although it supplies a strong argument *ab inconveniente* to such joinder."[1]

R. v. Owen, 1888, 20 QBD 829 was a case on which Mr Justice Charles was entitled to rely. The question arose on an indictment for an indecent assault which also contained a count for common assault. After the defendant gave evidence in his defence under the Criminal

---

1. *The Law Journal* - "The Legal Point Raised in the Wilde Case, 1895, vol.30, p.285, May 1895.

Law Amendment Act, 1885, Section 20 could he legally be convicted of a common assault only? Owen was acquitted of the charge of indecent assault but convicted of common assault.

Lord Coleridge CJ held that the conviction must be affirmed and continued:

> "The direction to the jury would, perhaps, have been more complete if the learned chairman had told them that the prisoner was only an admissible witness as to the indecent assault and had no right to give evidence as to the common assault which they must determine without reference as to his testimony ... It is true that there is no right to examine a prisoner on oath except on an indictment for a charge to which the Act applies, but it is also true that admissions made by a prisoner not on oath might always be received in evidence against him ... If in the course of giving evidence on oath, which the Act empowers him to do ... any admission or statement made by him in doing so must start on the footing of any other admission prior to the Act. The law gives the sanction of an oath to his statement so made, and it must be taken for or against him."

Lord Coleridge concluded his judgment by saying that in *R. v. Owen*, looking at the evidence without the prisoner's testimony, or with it, there was abundant evidence to support the conviction.

In its comments on *R. v. Wilde and Taylor, The Law Journal* drew attention to the difficulties raised and indicated the necessity of getting rid of the distinction between cases in which defendants could and those in which they could not testify. Because the counts on which the defendants could and could not give evidence were joined in the one indictment, if they gave evidence they were liable to be cross-examined on charges to which they were themselves debarred from giving evidence in chief if they went into the witness box.

This was remedied by the passing of the Criminal Law Amendment Act 1898. Defendants were competent but not compellable witnesses for all the charges they had to meet; and this has been the position now for over a hundred years.

At the close of the case for the prosecution in the first trial of *R. v. Wilde and Taylor*, the Crown withdrew the counts of conspiracy. As the jury disagreed on a number of counts of gross indecency, a retrial was ordered. On the retrial there were, of course, no counts of conspiracy for either Wilde or Taylor to face, and there were no counts on which they were jointly indicted. On a preliminary issue an application for their separate trials was therefore granted by Mr Justice Wills, the presiding Judge.

Evidence of an Accomplice

Contrary to the views of a number of friends of Oscar Wilde (eg, Frank Harris), Travers Humphreys, who had a junior brief in all three trials at the Old Bailey, expressed the opinion that when his client was indicted as a defendant:

> "On the whole, Wilde had little to complain of in the conduct of either of his trials. Both Charles J and Wills J were scrupulously fair to him, and he attained from both of these learned Judges rulings on the question of the corroboration of accomplices much more favourable than would be given in similar circumstances today (1948)."[2]

H. Montgomery Hyde, a barrister and an acknowledged expert on the trials, took the view that:

> "There can be little doubt that Wilde was justly convicted - indeed, he admitted as much himself to friends with whom he was in touch both during and after his imprisonment. The best that can be said for him is that, so far as is known, he never debauched any innocent young man. All his accomplices, on the strength of whose evidence he was condemned, were already

---

2. *The Trials of Oscar Wilde.* Ed. With Introduction by H. Montgomery Hyde. William Hodge 1948. Foreword by The Rt. Hon. Sir Travers Humphreys PC, p.4.

steeped in vice before Wilde met them, and two at least were notorious and self-confessed blackmailers."[3]

The Law Times of June 1, 1895 drew attention to the fact that while a conviction on the testimony of an accomplice was legal, the practice of Judges was almost invariably to advise juries not to convict upon the uncorroborated evidence of the accomplice. Furthermore, sometimes Judges, where the testimony of the accomplice was the only evidence, took it upon themselves to direct an acquittal.[4]

In the first trial Wilde and Taylor were tried together, with a single indictment containing 25 counts alleging the commission of acts of gross indecency by both men and conspiracy to procure such acts. In order to mount the trial the Crown offered immunity from prosecution to the young men with whom the alleged offences occurred, in return for their appearing as witnesses for the prosecution at the trial. These witnesses included Charles Parker, Frederick Atkins, Sidney Mavor, Alfred Wood and Edward Shelley. On oath Mavor denied that any impropriety had taken place and therefore there was no incriminating evidence to corroborate. That part of the case was therefore struck out. The first jury found Wilde not guilty of gross indecency with Shelley, but were unable to reach a verdict on the other counts. The corroboration was not provided by anyone who had seen the acts take place but by persons such as a masseur at the Savoy Hotel who gave evidence that he saw a young man in bed in Oscar Wilde's room; and by a chambermaid and the housekeeper who had noticed that the sheets of Wilde's bed had been "stained in a particular way". At both trials Sir Edward Clarke cross-examined the witnesses vigorously as to their recollections. In the second trial Wills J, in his summing-up, warned the jury to approach this evidence with caution. Furthermore, as the Judge regarded Atkins as an accomplice, he reminded the jury that his evidence should be corroborated. As there was no corroboration of the nature required by the law to warrant a conviction, the Judge

3. *Ibid.*, p.13.
4. The Legal Points in Wilde's Case. *The Law Times*. Vol.99, June 1, 1891, p.103.

withdrew that part of the case from the jury. Wilde was found guilty of gross indecency with Charles Parker, Alfred Wood and with a male person unknown.[5]

Little has changed in the last hundred years. Legal practitioners are reminded that in practice the prosecution must be careful before deciding to call as a witness an accomplice who is a participator in the crime of which the defendant is accused. Ordinarily this should not be done without a clear indication from the accomplice that he is willing to give evidence in favour of the Crown.[6]

In *MacDonald v. R.* (PCC) 1983 CAR Vol.77, 196 (a case from New Zealand), the Privy Council held that where an undertaking is given to an accomplice that there will be a stay of future proceedings, such an undertaking would always be honoured. Its practical importance lay in its practical effect on the state of mind of the accomplice giving evidence. Lord Diplock explained that:

> "The practice of making promises of this kind to accomplices, in order to remove or minimise the inducement to them to give false evidence exonerating themselves and inculpating the accused is of long standing in the administration of criminal justice in England - it dates back at least to 1775 in the time of Lord Mansfield."

Today, the Criminal Justice and Public Order Act 1994 32(1) applies and provides that:

> (1) Any requirement whereby at a trial on indictment it is obligatory for the court to give a warning about convicting the accused on the uncorroborated evidence of a person merely because the person is:
>
> (a)   an alleged accomplice of the accused, or
> (b)   where the offence charged is a sexual offence, the person

---

5. *The Trials of Oscar Wilde.* With introduction by H. Montgomery Hyde, p.74.
6. Archbold. *Criminal Proceeding. Evidence and Practice.* 1999 Edition. Sweet and Maxwell 1999, 4-194.

in respect of whom it is alleged to have been committed, is hereby abrogated ...

In *Makanjuola and E* 1995 CAR 469 the Court of Appeal held that it is a matter for the Judge's discretion what, if any, warning he considers appropriate in respect of an alleged accomplice or a complainant of a sexual offence, simply because a witness falls into one of those categories. Whether the Judge chooses to give a warning, and in what terms, will depend on the circumstances of the case, the issues raised and the quality of the witness's evidence.

This means that today the Judge's rulings concerning corroboration could be far less favourable to the accused than they were in 1895 or 1948. Lord Taylor LCJ in the *Makanjuola* case said that the Court of Appeal would be disinclined to interfere with a trial Judge's exercise of his discretion save in a case where that exercise is unreasonable.

Thus we see that a corroboration direction, which was previously obligatory, is no longer essential.

"The Last Word" in a Criminal Trial

The Solicitor-General, Sir Frank Lockwood, appeared for the Crown in the retrial. He was therefore able to exercise his right of reply and made the last speech on behalf of the prosecution to the jury, before the Judge's summing up, thus reversing the usual order. "The last word" to the jury has always been considered very important by barristers who have never underrated their own power of persuasion.[7] Sir Edward Clarke had to make his final speech before that of the Solicitor General; he bitterly complained, in his opening remarks on behalf of Wilde of the intended use of this privilege "which I myself when Solicitor-General never once exercised and will not exercise if ever I fill that distinguished position again ... Whether the defendant calls witnesses or not, the Solicitor-General

---

7. Jean Graham Hall and Gordon D. Smith. *R. v. Bywaters and Thompson*. Barry Rose Law Publishers Ltd. 1997, p.60.

enjoys the right - though why he should enjoy it I cannot imagine - of the last word with the jury."[8]

Today, neither the Attorney-General nor the Solicitor-General is granted such privilege. By the Criminal Procedure (Right of Reply) Act 1964 Section 1:

Upon the trial of any person on indictment:

(a)   the prosecution shall not be entitled to the right of reply on the grounds only that the Attorney-General or the Solicitor-General appears for the Crown at the trial.

(b)   the time at which the prosecution is entitled to exercise that right shall be, notwithstanding anything in Section 2 of the Criminal Procedure Act 1895, after the closing of the evidence for the defence and before the speech (if any) by or on behalf of the accused.

Thus, in all criminal trials today, at the end of the evidence for the defence, counsel for the Crown makes his closing speech, followed by counsel for the defendant.

---

8. H. Montgomery Hyde. *Oscar Wilde - A Biography*. Eyre Methuen. 1976, p.287.

CHAPTER 11

Prison - Then and Now

On Saturday, May 25, 1895, Oscar Wilde, having been found guilty of several offences under the Criminal Law Amendment Act 1885, was sentenced, together with his co-defendant Alfred Taylor, by Mr Justice Wills. Referring to the severest sentence the law allowed the Judge said: "In my judgment it is totally inadequate for such a case as this. The sentence of the court is that each of you be imprisoned and kept to hard labour for two years." The more knowledgeable listeners must have been particularly shocked: penal servitude would have been much preferable. Hard labour was usually in the prisoner's cell, where he would be in solitary confinement for 23 hours out of the 24, contrasting with the outdoor work in prisons such as Dartmoor. Even more shattering was the fact that there was no possibility of remission for good conduct: Oscar Wilde faced virtual incarceration for 730 days.

Following a weekend in the cells Wilde was driven to Pentonville, built on the grand scale in the 1840s for prisoners who lived north of the Thames. After the formalities at reception, including giving up all his personal belongings, he was told to strip and get into a bath where the water was already filthy, drying himself with a damp brown rag. As a member of the Home Office Committee investigating prisons Richard Burdon Haldane, QC, MP (later to become Lord Haldane, Lord Chancellor) was Oscar Wilde's first visitor in Pentonville on June 12, 1885. It is said that Margaret Brooke, the Ranee of Sarawak, an old friend of Wilde's, urged Haldane to go. When he visited the prison, Haldane was told by the Chaplain that Wilde was depressed and that he had refused to listen to any spiritual advice.[1] Haldane then saw Wilde alone in his cell. According to Haldane's autobiography:

> "At first he refused to speak. I put my hand on his prison-clad shoulder and said that I used to know him and that I had come to say something about himself. He had not fully used his great literary gift, and the reason was that he had lived a life of pleasure and had not made any great subject his own. Now misfortune might prove a blessing for his career for he had got a great subject. I would try to get him books and pen and ink, and in 18 months he would be free to produce. He burst into tears, and promised to make the attempt. For the books he asked eagerly saying that they would only give him *The Pilgrim's Progress* ... We hit on *St Augustine's Works* and on Momsen's *History of Rome*. These I got for him and they accompanied him from prison to prison."[2]

Although the authorities had intended that Oscar should complete his sentence at Pentonville he was transferred to Wandsworth prison for some unknown reason only six weeks later. This had been built a few years after Pentonville and was even larger, averaging 1,100 or so prisoners. Tragically the transfer proved to be even more traumatic. The food was even worse and some of the warders were brutal. "During the first six months I was dreadfully unhappy, so utterly miserable. I wanted to kill myself but what kept me from doing so was looking at the others and seeing that they were as unhappy as I was and feeling sorry for them."[3] Nevertheless his mental and physical condition deteriorated further. Haldane went to see Wilde in Wandsworth and found him quite crushed and broken. He was suffering from a fall which damaged his right ear. Haldane concluded that Wilde would be better off in Reading gaol

---

1. Jean Graham Hall and Douglas F. Martin. *Haldane - Statesman, Lawyer, Philosopher*. Barry Rose 1996, p.83.
2. Richard Burdon. *Haldane. An Autobiography*. Hodder and Stoughton. 1929, p.166.
3. *De Profundis*. Complete Works of Oscar Wilde, Harper Collins 1994.

and eventually the Governor suggested to the Prison Commissioners removal to a country prison.[4] That journey is most poignantly described in *De Profundis*:

"On November 13, 1895 I was brought down here from London. From two o'clock till half-past two on that day I had to stand on the centre platform of Clapham Junction in convict dress and handcuffed for the world to look at. I had been taken out of the Hospital Ward without a moment's notice being given to me. Of all possible objects I was the most grotesque. When people saw me they laughed. Each train as it came swelled the audience. Nothing could exceed their amusement. That was of course before they knew who I was. As soon as they had been informed they laughed still more. For half-an-hour I stood there in the grey November rain surrounded by a jeering mob."[5]

Reading was a small prison constructed on the lines of a miniature Pentonville. The building was laid down in the form of a cross, the administrative block being in the small transverse section with three cell blocks running into the large central area. The blocks, known as Galleries "A", "B" and "C" were on four floors, or landings. Wilde was put into cell 3 on the third landing of Gallery C, so that his prison number became "C.3.3." His life only marginally improved over the next eight months, principally due to the fact that the Governor, Major Isaacson, ran his institution on strict military lines. The slightest infringement of the many rules and regulations could lead to punishment, frequently in the form of reductions in food. The replacement of Major Isaacson by a new Governor, Major Nelson, brought more humane and thoughtful treatment for all prisoners and, in the last six months of his sentence, Oscar in particular. Books were now made available to him in greater numbers and even more importantly, writing materials. He was excused all forms of manual work and for the first time he felt he had enough to eat. He began to write again, mostly in the evenings,

---

4. *Haldane.* Jean Graham Hall and Douglas F. Martin, p.84.
5. *De Profundis.* Harper Collins. 1994, p.1040.

principally a long letter to Bosie, subsequently published as *De Profundis*. Despite his own attempts and those of several friends, including in particular More Adey and Frank Harris, as well as Bosie, he was not granted any remission. As the day of release approached, Major Nelson, noting Wilde's fear of press importuning, kindly arranged for him to leave early in the day and catch the London train from Twyford station, rather than Reading.

Comparison

Oscar's experience of prison is encapsulated in a letter that he wrote to the *Daily Chronicle*, published on March 24, 1898, some 10 months after his release. This had been triggered by the debate in the House of Commons on the second reading of the Prison Bill, that became the Prison Act later that year.

Wilde opined that the necessary reforms were very simple, concerning the needs of the body and the needs of the mind of each unfortunate prisoner. He explained: "With regard to the first, there are three punishments authorized by law in English prisons:

1 Hunger
2 Insomnia
3 Disease[6]"

1. *Prison fare*: Then as now, comprised three meals a day. In the 1890s breakfast consisted of cocoa or porridge, and eight ounces of brown (unbuttered) bread. The mid-day dinner was of bacon and beans with bread and potatoes, and either suet pudding or soup. (In another letter to the *Daily Chronicle* a few months earlier Oscar somewhat surprisingly described prison soup as "very good and wholesome"). One day a week cold meat was provided. At 6 pm, the evening meal: the prisoner had tea or gruel, together with another eight ounces of prison baked bread.

In *Introduction to Prisons and Imprisonment* Nick Flynn sets out a

---

6. Letter to *Daily Chronicle*, published March 24, 1898.

typical contemporary menu from Long Lartin prison in Worcestershire, a high security dispersal unit:

Breakfast: boiled egg, toast, marmalade or
              cereals, toast, marmalade or
              porridge, toast, marmalade.
Lunch: macaroni cheese or
              quiche or
              sausage roll
              (with potato/rice and bread)
Tea: vegetable stir fry or
              roast pork and gravy or
              braised liver and onions or
              french bread pizza.[7]

2. *Insomnia* was the inevitable consequence, in Oscar's view, of prisoners having to sleep on the plank bed they were supplied with at the outset; even though in course of time they were given a hard mattress, insomnia had by then become a habit. In fact, Oscar argued the whole object of the plank beds was to actually produce insomnia in the first place, which in his view invariably succeeded.

3. *By disease*, he meant the incessant diarrhoea which results from the prison diet coupled with the appalling sanitary "arrangements" in the cells. There had been latrines in cells in earlier years, but these had been removed after it was discovered that they had been used for - obviously illicit - communication.

Prisoners were issued with a tin chamber pot, but were only allowed to empty them during their exercise period. Worse, cell doors were locked at 5 pm and then could not be opened for any purpose whatsoever until the morning. The stench was compounded by an ineffective ventilation system and according to Oscar it was not uncommon for warders to be violently sick on opening cell doors. Curiously, it was to be 100 years before this repulsive practice was

---

7. Nick Flynn, *Introduction to Prisons and Imprisonment*. Waterside Press, 1998.

finally terminated, in 1996. Increasingly, throughout the 20th century "slopping out" became a flash-point for prisoners' grievances being cited as such in a number of riots. The practical alternative in most cases has been the installation of in-cell sanitary fittings, although this does, of course, reduce living space and also has an element of "living in a toilet".

Prison Doctors

The quality of prison doctors brought forth a scathing denunciation from Oscar:

"The officials who should not be allowed to hold any employment outside the prison or to have any private practice are the prison doctors.

At present the prison doctors have usually if not always a large prison practice and hold appointments in other institutions. The consequence is that the health of prisoners is entirely neglected and the sanitary condition of prisoners entirely overlooked. As a class I regard, and have always from my earliest youth regarded, doctors as by far the most humane profession in the community. But I must make an exception for prison doctors. They are, as far as I came across them and from what I saw in hospital and elsewhere, brutal in manner, coarse in temperament, and wholly indifferent to the health of the prisoners or their comfort."[8]

For some years there has been concern amongst penal reformers about the standards of professional competence of many prison doctors and a body of opinion that prison healthcare should be fully integrated with the National Health Service. The Government decided, however, that a more effective option would be a formal partnership between the NHS and the Prison Service, and the proposed basic structure was set out in a joint report published in

---

8. Letter to *Daily Chronicle*, published March 24, 1898.

the summer of 1999. The Prison Service will still be responsible for primary care in prisons but the NHS will assume responsibility for secondary care and specialist services. Doctors responsible for primary health care in prisons will in future be required to hold a certificate on post graduate training from the Joint Committee, whilst nurses will also have to be registered.

Mental Health

The main concern at grass roots level is the quality of mental health care in the prison system. Professor Pamela Taylor of the Institute of Psychiatry and Consultant to Broadmoor Special Hospital suggested, in an interview with Michael Simmons, that out of a prison population of 65,000, possibly as many as 25,000 could have mental disorders. She emphasised that they vary from category to category, and whilst not all need to be in a hospital, many would benefit from specialist help.[9]

In the House of Commons debate on Prison Health Service, on March 19, 1998, Helen Jones, MP, said: "... of the 195 doctors employed in the prison service only 21 are members of the Royal College of Psychiatry or hold a diploma in psychiatric medicine ... Only 21 per cent of all health care officials and nursing grades employed in the prisons are registered mental nurses."[10]

The biggest element in mental health is substance misuse and addiction, not only with prisoners but for some prison officers. The practical difficulties of control are immense, but this is not the place to attempt any analysis or discussion of a universal social problem.

Principal Needs of Prisoners

Oscar also suggested that the three principal needs of the mind for prisoners where reforms were essential were:

---

9. *Howard League Magazine*, August, 1998.
10. *Hansard HC*, vol.308, col.1512.

1. Books
2. Visits
3. Letters.

1. Books

In 1895 a prisoner was only permitted three books during the first three months of imprisonment, ie, the Bible, Prayer Book and Hymn Book. Then he was allowed to borrow one book per week from the prison library; but Oscar scathingly dismissed most of the stock as third rate, badly written religious books chosen by the Prison Chaplain.

At the beginning of the 21st century it is facile to assume that literacy is much greater than in Wilde's time but it is a salutary fact that many prisoners today are on entry illiterate. In the November 1999 issue of the *Prison Reform Trust* magazine the Director General of the Prison Service explained:

> "Between 60 and 70 per cent (of prisoners) have such poor basic literacy and numeracy skills that they are ineligible for 96 per cent of jobs. I have, therefore, made improving basic and key skills a priority ..."

Education at all levels is now encouraged but basic literacy teaching is reinforced by outside volunteers and by other prisoners, provided they hold Basic Literacy Teaching Certificates. Prison libraries today aim to provide a comprehensive service as near as possible to outside libraries, stocking foreign language books, magazines and newspapers, cassettes and games.

2. Visits

Oscar was allowed only four visits a year limited to 20 minutes each: moreover, except in the case of the prisoner's legal representative, both he and the visitor were placed in a large wooden or iron cage, having a small aperture covered with wire netting. Two warders stood between the cages, with freedom to listen or even stop or interrupt the conversation if they felt so inclined.

The inhumanity inherent in such a system enraged both Bosie and Oscar. In Douglas's *Autobiography* he wrote: "The visitor and the prisoner have to shout to make their voices heard above the voices of the other prisoners and visitors. Nothing more revolting and cruel and deliberately malignant could be devised by human ingenuity. Poor Oscar was rather deaf. He could hardly hear what I said in the babel. He looked at me with tears running down his cheeks and I looked at him." Oscar's outrage was obvious from his letter to the *Daily Chronicle*: "To be exhibited like an ape in a cage to people who are fond of one is a needless and horrible degradation."[11] Wilde argued that such interviews should take place in the same conditions in which a prisoner was allowed to see his solicitor, that is to say in a room with a glass door, on the other side of which stood a warder.

The Prison Service now fully acknowledges the vital importance of maintaining links with the family, and permits visiting as often as circumstances allow. The minimum is two visits of one hour duration every month for convicted prisoners (with extra permitted for good behaviour) and to those on remand one-and-a-half hours of visits each week. In contrast to Oscar's experience Governors may allow special visits from legal advisers which are outside the minimum entitlement.

3. Letters

Wilde was also limited to writing four letters a year, which he naturally felt could not properly sustain feelings of affection. He also complained of the "mutilating and expurgating" of prisoner's letters. The modern Prison Service distinguishes between convicted and remand prisoners in this instance, setting limits on the mail the former may send or receive but with no restrictions for those on remand. Censorship remains however, as Nick Flynn explains. Incoming mail is searched as a matter of routine and may be read by the staff. Exceptions to this are letters sent to or received from solicitors or the Prison Ombudsman.

---

11. Lord Alfred Douglas. *Autobiography*. Martin Secker. 1929.

Homosexuality in Prison

After Oscar's initial rage on being imprisoned had abated, he was overcome by feelings of total despair. Gradually, in his second year, he responded to what he described as the really humanising influence of other prisoners (as well as the approaches from those wardens who were well disposed towards him). According to H. Montgomery Hyde, despite the ban on conversation during the exercise period, Wilde was able to get to talk to them and "... eventually he knew each one's name and history and date of his release."[12] There is no record of any homosexual involvements but this would have been extremely difficult if not impossible in the then prison conditions, even if Wilde were minded to have an affaire.

In the 21st century, the "love that dares not speak its name" is now free to do so, even if not completely untrammelled in prison. In an article in the June 2000 edition of the monthly gay magazine *Axiom* the author, Philip Scott, states: "Recent Home Office figures put the number of 'out' gay prisoners at 3,701, about five per cent of the total male inmate population" - but adds "... many gay inmates prefer to remain anonymous." Clearly there are special problems for gay men in prison, as evidenced by the founding in 1997 of the first gay support charity, Out-Side-In, better known as OSI. Mr Scott highlights one in particular: "One of the problems prisoners have to face is the underlying suspicion or assumption that all gay prisoners are sex offenders or paedophiles. The reality is that there are more gay people in prison for theft, GBH or fraud than sex offences."

Conclusion

At first glance a comparison of the principal problems of the prison service between 1895 and 2000 depressingly seem to show only limited real progress. Overcrowding is in general as real as ever, but now the root causes of this are the rapidly rising prison population,

---

12. H. Montgomery Hyde: *Oscar Wilde - the Aftermath*, Methuen, 1963.

swollen by remand - which currently accounts for 20 per cent of the total of approximately 68,000 (including 3,000+ women). Chris Duffin, the Overcrowding Monitor of the Prison Reform Trust points out that the numbers in each prison do affect the quality of the regimes within. He explains: "The training prisons' regimes are usually based on fixed numbers, but the local prisons where a large number of short-term prisoners serve the whole of their sentence are very poorly served in programmes and activities." Brutality of prison officers is still in question; at the time of writing, no less than 27 from Wormwood Scrubs have been suspended pending investigation. Recidivism, ie, reoffending, seems substantially unchanging over the years: it may be that to think of a substantial reduction is simply unrealistic.

However, there are grounds for cautious optimism. The Woolf Report of 1991 is now being gradually implemented after some early "hiccups". At the present time the treatment of young offenders is receiving most of the attention: in Oscar's day it seems very few people were even aware of the problems. His other main concerns - hospital doctors, prison diet, beds, work and association are now based on more humane approaches. Casting a huge shadow over the whole of the penal system today is the enormous problem of drug abuse.

OSCAR WILDE: Daily Routine		*2000 Typical Daily Routine*	
0600	Clean cell and "slop out"	0730	Prisoners are woken up by the officers and their cells unlocked. Breakfast is served
0700	Breakfast		
0730	Exercise (1 hour)		
0830	Work	0820	Those prisoners who work or attend education are allowed off the wing for exercise
0900	Work	0900	Work and education classes begin. Those who are unemployed are locked in their cells

1100	Work	1110	Those who are unemployed are unlocked and have an opportunity to leave the wing for exercise
1200	Dinner	1210	By this time all prisoners must return to the wing
1230	Work	1315	Lunch is served
1300	Work	1340	All prisoners are locked in their cells and officers check the roll (numbers)
		1400	Those going to work or education are unlocked. Prisoners who have a visit planned will be unlocked when the wing is notified that their visitors have arrived. They are then taken to the visits room. Other prisoners remain locked in their cells.
1600	Work	1600	Visits end
1700	Work	1700	All prisoners are now back on the wing. They will be locked in their cells and the roll checked
1800	Tea	1750	Prisoners are unlocked and tea is served
1800	Lights out: bed	1830	Evening activities begin. This usually means access to television, pool tables, table football and recreation with other prisoners. Some prisoners will have the opportunity to go to the gymnasium
		2000	Prisoners who have attended activities off the wing must return
		2020	Prisoners are locked up for the night. Officers do the final check of the roll

(With acknowledgements to the Howard League for Penal Reform.)

The Human Rights Act 1998 came into effect on October 2, 2000. We are sure that Oscar Wilde if he were alive today would be the first to query whether it would make any difference to the prisoner's lot.

"But this I know, that every law
That men hath made for man,
Since first man took his brother's life,
And the sad world began,
But straws the wheat and saves the chaff,
With a most evil fan.

This too I know - and wise it were
If each could know the same -
That every prison that men build
Is built with bricks of shame,
And bound with bars lest Christ should see
How men their brothers maim."

From *The Ballad of Reading Gaol*[13]

---

13. Oscar Wilde. *The Ballad of Reading Gaol*. Smithers 1898.

Bibliography

Archbold. *Criminal Pleading Evidence and Practice.* Ed. Sweet and Maxwell.

Aronson, Theo. *Prince Eddy and the Homosexual Underworld.* John Murray. 1994.

Bartlett, Neil. *Who was that man?* Serpents Tail. 1988.

Bowley, Martin QC. "An Overdue Reform". *New Law Journal.* Vol. 149. Butterworths.

Chambers. *Biographical Dictionary 5th Ed.* Chambers. 1990.

Church of England Moral Welfare Council. *The Problem of Homosexuality.* Church Information Board. 1953.

Douglas, Lord Alfred. *Oscar Wilde and Myself.* John Long. 1914.

Douglas, Lord Alfred. *Autobiography.* Martin Secker. 1929.

Flynn, Nick. *Introduction to Prison and Imprisonment.* Waterside Press. 1998.

Gardiner, Gerald QC and Martin, Andrew (Ed.). *Law Reform Now.* Gollancz. 1963.

Gibbs, A.M. (Ed.). *Shaw Interviews and Recollections.* University of Iowa Press. 1990.

Graham Hall, J. and Martin, D.F. *Haldane - Statesman, Lawyer, Philosopher.* Barry Rose Law Publishers. 1996.

Graham Hall, J. and Smith, Gordon D.R. *R. v. Bywaters and Thompson.* Barry Rose Law Publishers. 1991.

Harris, Frank (preface by Bernard Shaw). *Oscar Wilde*. Constable. 1938.

Holyroyd, Michael. *Bernard Shaw. Vol. 1. The Search for Love*. Chatto and Windus. 1998.

Hyde, Montgomery H. *The Trials of Oscar Wilde*. (Ed.). William Hodge. 1948.

Hyde, Montgomery H. *Oscar Wilde - the Aftermath*. Methuen. 1963.

Hyde, Montgomery H. *Oscar Wilde - A Biography*. Methuen. 1976.

Krafft-Ebing, Dr. Richard von. *Psychopathia Sexualis*. Paperback Library Inc. 1965.

Law Commission. *Working Paper No. 84 Criminal Libel*. HMSO. 1982.

Millard, Christopher S. *Oscar Wilde - Three Times Tried*. Ferrestone Press. 1912.

Morley, Sheridan. *Oscar Wilde*. Weidenfeld and Nicolson. 1976.

Mort, Professor Frank. *Mapping Sexual London. Sexual Geographies No. 37*. Lawrence and Wishart. 1999.

Page, Norman. *An Oscar Wilde Chronology*. Macmillan. 1991.

Pearson, Heskett. *The Life of Oscar Wilde*. Methuen. 1946.

Penison, William A. *Homosexuality in Modern France*. (Ed.). OUP. 1996.

Poldy, Michael S. *The Trials of Oscar Wilde*. Yale University Press. 1997.

Report of the Committee on Homosexual Offences and Prostitution. Cmnd. 247. HMSO. 1957.

Report of the Committee on Defamation. Cmnd. 5909. HMSO. 1975.

Report of the Supreme Court Procedure Committee on Practice and Procedure in Defamation. 1991.

Rostow, Prof. Eugene V. "The Enforcement of Morals". *Cambridge Law Journal*. Stevens. 1960.

Schmidgall, Gary. *The Stranger Wilde*. Dutton. 1994.

Shaw, George Bernard. *Dark Lady of the Sonnets*. 1914.

Sibalis, Michael David. *The Regulation of Male Homosexuality in Revolutionary and Napoleonic France 1789-1815. Homosexuality in Modern France.* OUP. 1996.

Sinfield, Alan. *The Wilde Century.* Cassell. 1994.

Weeks, Jeffery. *Coming Out - Homosexual Politics in Britain from the Nineteenth Century to the Present Day.* Quartet Books. 1977.

Weeks, Jeffery. *Sex, Politics and Society.* 2nd Edn. Longman. 1989.

Wilde, Oscar. *The Ballad of Reading Gaol.* Smithers. 1898.

Wilde, Oscar. *De Profundis.* Methuen. 1905. *Complete Works of Oscar Wilde.* Harper Collins. 1994.

Wildeblood, Peter. *Against the Law.* Weidenfeld and Nicolson. 1955.

Wilson, Colin. *Written in Blood.* Grafton Books. 1990.